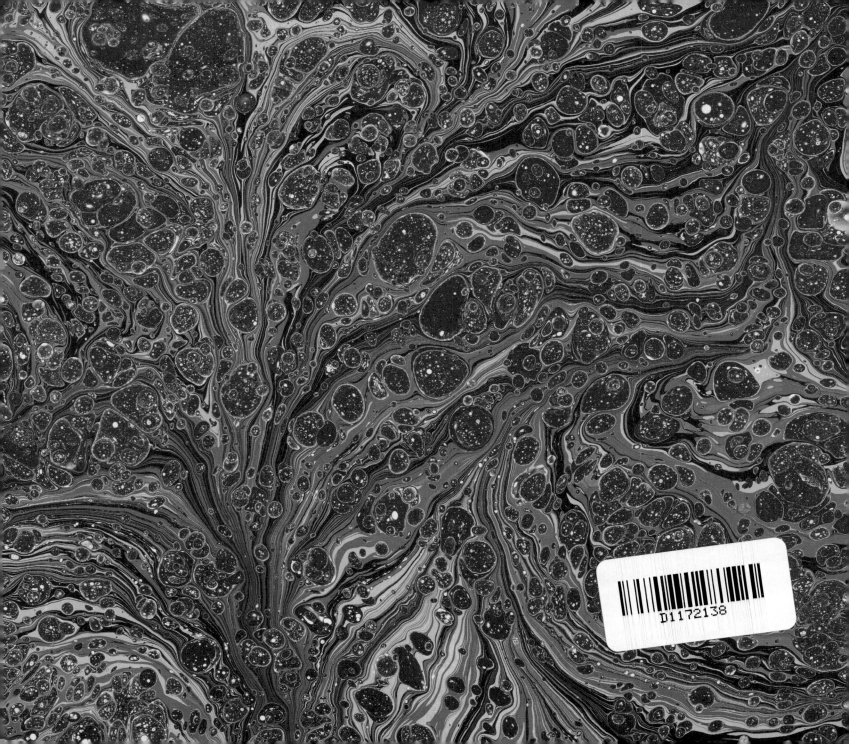

Tomáš Jakl | Bernard Panuš | Jiří Tintěra

CZECHOSLOVAK ARMORED CARS
IN THE FIRST WORLD WAR AND THE RUSSIAN CIVIL WAR

Schiffer Publishing Ltd

4880 Lower Valley Road • Atglen, PA 19310

Type set in Helvetica Neue LT Pro/Minion Pro

ISBN: 978-0-7643-4804-4
Printed in China

Published by Schiffer Publishing, Ltd.
4880 Lower Valley Road
Atglen, PA 19310
Phone: (610) 593-1777; Fax: (610) 593-2002
E-mail: Info@schifferbooks.com

For our complete selection of fine books on this and related subjects, please visit our website at www.schifferbooks.com.
You may also write for a free catalog.

This book may be purchased from the publisher.
Please try your bookstore first.

We are always looking for people to write books on new and related subjects. If you have an idea for a book, please contact us at proposals@schifferbooks.com.

Schiffer Publishing's titles are available at special discounts for bulk purchases for sales promotions or premiums. Special editions, including personalized covers, corporate imprints, and excerpts can be created in large quantities for special needs. For more information, contact the publisher.

CONTENTS

ACKNOWLEDGMENTS

The chapters on Czechoslovak armored cars in Russia would never have come into existence without the kind help of the following (in alphabetical order); to whom the authors of this text express their sincere thanks: Daniela Brádlerová, Ludmila Kakušková, Katya Kocourek, Jana Nalezencová, and Viera Žižková; and: Jaroslav Čvančara, Zdeněk Grepl, Pavel Holý, Radan Lášek, Oleg Ruboš, Robert Speychal, Karel Straka, Petr Štěpánek, and Jan Vaněk. Special thanks also go to Bernard Panuš, whose photo of the JANOŠÍK armored car inspired the whole project several years ago.

The chapters on the armored cars of the Czechoslovak Army in Italy came about thanks to Lieutenant Colonel Joseph Hranáč, the deputy commander of the pre-WWII Tank Battalion, and author of the battalion's chronicle, Private František Marek, from pre-WWII Armored Car Company; and Sergeant Josef Dvořák, deputy commander of the armored car No. 2 and witness to events in Slovakia during the war with Hungary. And thanks also, although unnamed here on request, the relatives of an officer of a pre-WWII 1st Tank Regiment, who in 1939, hid the Regiment's chronicle against German occupiers. Much of this work involved was based on conversations and advice from Pavel Minařík, Pavel Šrámek and the distinguished historian of Slovak history Marian Hronský. Jaroslav Tvrdý kindly provided information pertaining to Hungarian vessels.

The Diphrology Club and the authors welcome any additional information about the appearance and fate of the vehicles described in this book.

The book was prepared with the kind support of following institutions:

Vojenský historický ústav
Military History Institute

Vojenský ústřední archiv
Central Military Archive

Klub přátel pplk. Karla Vašátky
Colonel Karel Vašátko Friends Club

Difrologický klub
Diphrology Club

Československá obec legionářská
Czechoslovak Legionnaires Community

INTRODUCTION

The volunteer units of the Czechoslovak Army in Exile were one of the basic pillars and conditions for the establishment and international recognition of an independent Czechoslovakia on 28th October 1918. These complemented the diplomatic actions undertaken by the group of Czechoslovaks in political exile centered around Professor Tomáš Garrigue Masaryk, as well as the political actions of Czech and Slovak MPs and politicians in Austria-Hungary, who also received support from Czechoslovak expatriate communities around the world.

The basis of the Czechoslovak Army in Russia, the Czech Druzhina, was founded in Kiev on 12th August 1914. Its four original companies were composed of Czechs living in Russia before the war. Soon other companies were created, composed of Czechs and Slovaks, who crossed the front. The Druzhina's units were allocated to the various Russian divisions as intelligence companies and half-companies. In 1916, from the Czech Druzhina a regiment emerged and soon after a brigade with two and then with three regiments.

In the summer of 1917, the Czechoslovak Brigade units were concentrated in Galicia and the brigade as a whole participated in the Russian Kerensky Offensive. After winning the battle at Zborov on 2nd July 1917 and covering the retreat of the Russian Army Group of General Erdelli, the brigade was sent to Polonoye, southwest of Kiev, for replenishment. The influx of Czechoslovak volunteers from Russian POW camps enabled the creation of a new, 2nd Czechoslovak Rifle Division in Borispol on 26th July 1917, and also the transformation of the Czechoslovak Brigade into the 1st Czechoslovak Rifle Division on 19th September 1917. Two thousand volunteers went away to

Czech Druzhina leaving to the front in Galicia in 1914. The Laurin & Klement car of Czech origin was donated to the Druzhina by Mr. L.V. Tuček, director of the L & K factory head office for the Russian market in Moscow. *Courtesy of VÚA-VHA*

Laurin & Klement car of the Czech Druzhina in Galicia in the winter of 1914/1915. *Courtesy of VÚA-VHA*

in Darney, France, on 22nd June 1918. The Brigade in the French 53rd Infantry Division fought in October 1918 at Vouziers. After the First World War the Czechoslovak Brigade was reorganized into the 5th Rifle Division on 5th December 1918 and returned to the newly created Czechoslovak Republic.

In Italy, identical to the situation in Russia, Czechoslovak reconnaissance troops were the first to appear. In the spring of 1918, the Italian government allowed the creation of military units from prisoners of Czech and Slovak origin. Gradually six Rifle Regiments were created and merged into the 6th Rifle Division at Foligno on 23rd April 1918. Starting in August 1918, the division was deployed at Monte Baldo, and participated in the battle for Doss Alto on 21st September 1918. After the

strengthen the Czechoslovak regiments in France. Both divisions were merged into the Czechoslovak Rifle Corps on 9th October 1917, which at the turn of 1917-1918 numbered about 45,000 men. After the outbreak of the Russian Civil War in November 1917, the Czechoslovak Corps declared neutrality in matters of Russian domestic policy and began negotiating a move from Russia to France.

In France the Czech Company "Rota Nazdar" was created within the French Foreign Legion on 31st August 1914. The arrival of volunteers from Romania, Russia, Italy, and the USA in the spring of 1918 allowed the creation of three rifle regiments, which were merged into the Czechoslovak Brigade

Prvni český automobil 2.hé roty zhotovený v Kijevě.

The first car of the second company. Cartoon from 1914. *Courtesy of Jiří Charfreitag*

CZECHOSLOVAK ARMORED CARS IN THE FIRST WORLD WAR AND THE RUSSIAN CIVIL WAR

First World War, the 6th Rifle Division was reorganized into the Czechoslovak Army Corps with the 6th and 7th Rifle Divisions in Padua on 17th November 1918. The Corps returned to Czechoslovakia in December 1918. Besides the Czechoslovak Army Corps, which was created from men who volunteered prior to the end of war, numerous Czechoslovak Home Guard battalions were created in Italy. Former soldiers of the Austro-Hungarian Army of Czech and Slovak origin, disarmed after the armistice, belonged to the Home Guard.

The motorization of armies in the First World War was in its infancy, and horses were a fairly basic and widespread means of transportation. Railroads were already playing a strategic role in the wars of the second half of the nineteenth century, while automobiles, however, only later assumed an important place in the thinking of the military authorities. Armored vehicles were created during the First World War.

At the end of the war, Czechoslovak legions were motorized at an advanced level. In France, where it was not possible to replenish the military from Czech and Slovak prisoners of war, because the Austro-Hungarian Army was not present on the Western Front, Czechoslovak regiments remained dependent on automobile units of the French Army. In contrast, in Italy, the Czechoslovak Corps has several hundred cars and trucks. In battles involving the Czechoslovak legions during the Civil War in Russia, and in the vast spaces

Czechoslovak Brigade in France, car Ford T in Seutheim, France. *Courtesy of VÚA-VHA*

Exercise of Czechoslovak Legionnaires in France with dummy tanks, St. Maixent, September and October 1918. *Courtesy of Josef Turek*

Another dummy tank, this time even horse-drawn, St. Étienne, France, 1918. *Courtesy of VÚA-VHA*

In the camp of the Czechoslovak Brigade in Mourmelon: the French Legionnaires photographed a French St. Chamond tank chassis, which was used as a heavy prime mover. *Courtesy of VÚA-VHA*

The recruitment camp of Czechoslovak volunteers in Stamford, USA, had a Ford T Woody Wagon car. *Courtesy of VÚA-VHA*

Ford T car in Stamford in front of the camp office, where a reading room and warehouse were located, as well as a tailor and shoemaker. *Courtesy of VÚA-VHA*

Truck park of Czechoslovak Army Corps in Italy, Castelfranco, Italy on 28 October 1918. *Courtesy of VÚA-VHA*

General Maurice Janin, supreme commander of allied expeditionary forces in Siberia, 1918-1919. *Courtesy of VÚA-VHA*

of Siberia, both armored trains and trains with residential carriages gained particular notoriety.

Legionary armored cars undeservedly remain in the shadow of other weapons, especially armored trains. The number and extent of the combat deployment of "bronyeviki" on wheels cannot be compared with "bronyeviki" on rails. On closer inspection, however, it is clear that in this case these were an important means of fighting, which accompanied the legionaries in all key battles from the beginning to the end of their Siberian adventure, and also in the struggle for Slovakia.

Memorial of Czechoslovak soldiers on the Maritime cemetery in Vladivostok. *Courtesy of VÚA-VHA*

CHAPTER 1

ARMORED CARS OF THE CZECHOSLOVAK LEGIONS IN RUSSIA, 1918-1920

1914-1917 THE FIRST ENCOUNTER WITH THE NEW WEAPON

Czechoslovak volunteers in the Russian Army became acquainted with armored cars in the First World War. In 1915, in Tarnopol, at headquarters of the Russian 11th Army, they photographed the heavy armored car Garford named PUSHKAR (ПУШКАРЬ), and the Austin armored cars first series, named PYLKIY (ПЫЛКЫЙ) and ROBYEDA (ПОБѣДА), which belonged to the Russian 19th automobile machine gun platoon. In Galicia they also came across armored cars Mors and Renault of the Belgian armored car section (Corps des Autos-Canons-Mitrailleuses, ACM), which were deployed on the Russian side after 1915. The Belgian armored car section was deployed in Galicia in 1916, for the Russian 6th Corps of the 11th Army. The headquarters of this section was in Ozerna, near Zborov, Ukraine. In June 1917, before the Russian summer Kerensky Offensive, the Czechoslovak Rifle Brigade was based at Zborov. The Czechoslovaks and the Belgians soon became friends and

Heavy armored Garford PUSHKAR of the Russian 19th automobile machine-gun platoon in Tarnopol, 1915. *Courtesy of VÚA-VHA*

Two other vehicles of the 19th automobile machine gun platoon were machine-gun armored cars Austin first series PYLKIY …

… and POBEDA. *Both courtesy of VÚA-VHA*

Unidentified Garford heavy armored car with members from a Russian Army headquarters. *Author's collection*

Evacuation of a wounded member of the Czech Druzhina from the first-line with an armored car, Austin first series. *Courtesy of VÚA-VHA*

Rail transport of the 15th automobile machine gun platoon of the Russian Army in unknown location. On the right is the Austin first series ADSKIY, followed by another Austin first series with an improvised reduced roof cab and a Lanchester armored car behind it. This photo created the myth of the armored car ADSKIY service in the Czechoslovak Legions. *Courtesy of VÚA-VHA*

played football matches against each other. They also arranged a match in Lviv following the victorious offensive. Although the Czechoslovak Brigade conquered all three Austro-Hungarian trenches in an attack on 2nd July 1917 near Zborov, which made them famous, the overall Russian offensive was a failure. Therefore a proposed Czechoslovak-Belgian football match in Lviv did not take place.

Neither the Czech Druzhina, the Czechoslovak Rifle Regiment nor the Czechoslovak Rifle Brigade had any armored vehicles in their possession during 1914-1917. Only after the organization of the Czechoslovak Rifle Corps, created as a result of the success at Zborov on 9th October 1917, did it come into the possession of armored cars. However, because of the development of events in Russia, the Corps had no officially assigned armored vehicles.

In 1917, Russia, exhausted by war, began to crumble. The Revolution in March 1917 (according to the calendar in use at that time, dated February)

Fighting on the Western Front was suspended in stalemate positional battles, from which there was no way out. On the eastern front therefore a Belgian armored car section was deployed for which there was greater application than in Flanders fields. The images show a Belgian armored cars section (ACM, French: Corps Belge Auto Cannons Mitrailleuses, Flemish: Korps Autos-Canons-Mitrailleuse) being inspected by Chief of Staff of the Russian 9th Army of the southwestern front, Lieutenant General Shishkevich in Volochinsk, January 1916. *Courtesy of VÚA-VHA*

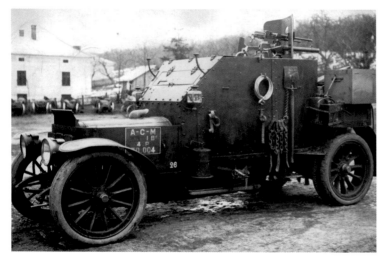

Belgian armored cars, Mors, Zbarazh, April 1916. *Courtesy of VÚA-VHA*

Mobile workshop of Belgian armored car section. *Courtesy of VÚA-VHA*

Command version of the Mors armored car. *Courtesy of VÚA-VHA*

forced the abdication of Tsar Nicholas II. The newly established Russian Republic was defeated in November (according to the Russian calendar, in October) of that year by Lenin's faction of the Russian Social Democratic Party (whose members called themselves Bolsheviks, and then, from March 8th, 1918, also Communists), in a coup funded by the German Emperor Wilhelm II. The Bolsheviks, in return for financial assistance from the German Empire, immediately signed an armistice with Germany, Austro-Hungary and Turkey. In free elections, held in December 1917, the Bolsheviks overwhelmingly lost. They disregarded the results of the elections and began to systematically destroy their political opponents. The country plunged into civil war. Finland, Estonia, Lithuania, Poland, Ukraine, Siberia, Caucasus, and Central Asia broke away from the Russian Empire and declared independence. The Russian Army on the front started falling apart and was partly disbanded by the Bolsheviks. At the beginning of 1918, German and Austro-Hungarian troops launched an unexpected attack to the east, which the disintegrated Russian Army and weak Red Guard units were unable to deflect. As a result, the Central Powers occupied the Baltic states, Belarus, Poland, and Ukraine.

The Czechoslovak Corps, whose troops were still at that time considered part of the Entente Powers, had to leave Ukraine before the German advance. The rearguard of the Corps, consisting of the 1st and 4th Rifle Regiment, marched

Belgian soldiers and members from the headquarters of the Russian 11th Army in front of a church in Zbarazh. *Courtesy of VÚA-VHA*

Belgian soldiers in Zbarazh. *Courtesy of VÚA-VHA*

Belgian soldiers in Zbarazh. *Courtesy of VÚA-VHA*

Czechoslovak and Belgian soldiers in a train station in the Baranovichi-Pinsk area. A small cross marks, later general, Husák. *Courtesy of VÚA-VHA*

from Zhytomyr in the direction of Kiev on 24th February 1918. One day later, on 25th February 1918, at the request of local residents in Korostyshev, the Czechoslovaks decided not to blow up a stone bridge over the Teterev River. Two German armored cars took advantage of this action, and attacked the Czechoslovak rearguard, which consisted of sergeant Musílek's reconnaissance group and the 3rd Battalion of the 1st Rifle Regiment, between Korostyshev and the village of Tsarevka.

This was the very first combat engagement involving Czechoslovak soldiers with enemy armored vehicles during the war. Two armored cars of unknown type marked with black crosses on their turrets and Ukrainian flags were able to approach the immediate vicinity where Czechoslovak soldiers were on the march. They opened fire when overtaking. The legionaries took cover in drains and in the woods that lined both sides of the road, and with hand grenades and rifle fire drove away both armored cars. On the road there remained only horses harnessed in machine-gun carts. After the clash Czechoslovak soldiers blocked the road with fallen trees and telegraph poles. In the skirmish two legionaries were killed from sergeant Musílek's reconnaissance group: František Petr and Karel Valenta, who were buried in Tsarevka. Four other legionnaires were wounded, one of whom, Karel Šteiger, also from sergeant Musílek's reconnaissance group, died a few hours later the following day, he was buried with military honors in the village of Stavishtche. According to survey reports, three Germans died in the armored vehicles, including one staff officer. These armored vehicles were either from the 1st Machine Gun Section of Armored Cars or the 2nd Machine-Gun Section of Armored Cars.

Soldiers of the 1st Czechoslovak Reserve Battalion during the retreat through Korostyshev, Ukraine, February 1918. *Courtesy of VÚA-VHA*

German armored car Ehrhardt E-V/4 belonging to 2nd machine-gun armored car platoon, Kiev, March 1918. National markings were black pattée crosses on white square fields on the turret. A black shaded white numeral "2" on the bonnet probably indicated the number of the platoon. *Courtesy of VHÚ*

The sole built German Büssing model 1915 armored car, in service with the 1st machine gun armored car section. *Courtesy of VHÚ*

Bridge across the Teterev River at Korostyshev, Ukraine. On 25 February 1918, in the woods behind the rearguard, Czechoslovak Army Corps had their first encounter with two German armored cars. It was the first known combat engagement of Czechoslovak soldiers with enemy armored vehicles during the war. *Courtesy of VÚA-VHA*

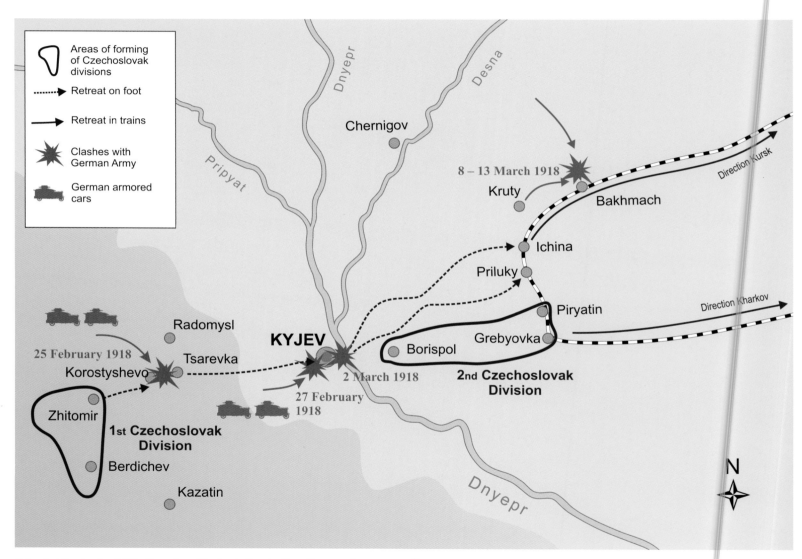

Retreat of Czechoslovak Rifle Corps from Ukraine to Russia. *Hana Rozmanitá, courtesy of ČSOL*

Bolshevik takeover in Priluki, 10th March 1918. The man in the hat and with a pipe is Dr. J. Persić from the American YMCA mission to the Czechoslovak Army Corps in Russia. On his left is an Austin third series. *Courtesy of VÚA-VHA*

a little white, black-shaded number two on the front engine, and a white rectangle with a black number "DB 5681." Bright, maybe all white, without any marking, was the sole exemplar of the armored car Ehrhardt E-V/4 model 1915 of the 1st Machine Gun Section of Armored Cars.

Further engagement between German armored cars and Czechoslovak legionaries occurred on 27th February. In the village of Ignatovka near Kiev the rearguard of the 3rd Czechoslovak Rifle Regiment was attacked by two German armored cars. Between 6th and 11th March, Czechoslovak Rifle Corps fought against the German 91st and 214th Infantry Divisions, 2nd Cavalry Division and parts of the 45th Territorial Division at the Bakhmach railway junction, through which ran the evacuation of the Corps to the east. In these battles armored cars are not mentioned.

Both of these units were transported via railway to Kovel on 19th February 1918. From there they were driven on to Luck, where they were subordinate to the German 2nd Cavalry Division. One day later, on 20th February, they went through Rovno, Zhitomir and Novogradvolynsk to Kiev, which they reached on 5th March 1918.

In February 1918, the German 1st Machine Gun Section of Armored Cars (Panzerkraftwagen-MG-Abteilung 1) had one reconnaissance vehicle, a Daimler Maschinengewehrwagen 1914, and four armored cars: Daimler model 1915, Ehrhardt E-V/4 model 1915, Ehrhardt E-V/4 model 1917, and Büssing A5P model 1915 (as a backup). The 2nd Machine-Gun Platoon of Armored Cars (Panzerkraftwagen-MG-Zug 2) had two armored Ehrhardt E-V/4 model 1917s. Some German machines were painted white, according to the recollections of some legionaries. On surviving photos the armored cars Ehrhardt E-V/4 model 1917 are painted gray, with white and black rimmed squares on the turrets, and a black cross pattée. In another photo taken in Kiev the Ehrhardt E-V/4 model 1917 of the 2nd Machine-Gun Platoon of Armored Cars also had

Soldiers of the 5th Czechoslovak Rifle Regiment handed over their weapons to the Bolsheviks in Penza, Russia, March 1918. *Courtesy of VÚA-VHA*

SPRING AND SUMMER 1918 – CONFLICT WITH THE BOLSHEVIKS

By signing the Treaty of Brest-Litovsk on 3rd March 1918, defeated Russia became a vassal of the Central Powers, and paid reparations, and supplied raw materials and agricultural products. The Czechoslovak legions and the Russian government, represented by the People's Commissar for Nationalities, Josef Stalin, concluded an agreement, according to which the legionaries would be able to leave for France via Vladivostok. The legion was obliged to remain neutral in Russia's internal political affairs and to deliver a majority of the weapons in its possession, but those guarding the transportation of trains could still hold some weapons. Disarmament took place in Penza, from where transportation continued on the Trans-Siberian Railway further east. In Penza the Czechoslovak regiment of the Red Army was also formed. In late April 1918, the Czechoslovak transportation route, under pressure from Germany, came to a halt. Priority was given to the transportation of German and Austro-Hungarian prisoners repatriated from Russian POW camps. German Emperor Wilhelm II and the Austrian Emperor Karl I sent a telegram on 28th April 1918, which ordered all Germans and Austrians in Russia to work

Wagons of the 5th Czechoslovak Rifle Regiment standing at Penza train station in April 1918. *Courtesy of VÚA-VHA*

Czechoslovak legionaries with sticks instead of arms in the spring of 1918. *Courtesy of VÚA-VHA*

Czechoslovaks on the balcony of the hotel Dadinniy, which had previously served as the local Soviet prison, in Chelyabinsk, 28th May 1918. *Courtesy of VÚA-VHA*

for Vladivostok, regardless of orders from Lenin's government. On 25th May 1918, Trotsky responded with a telegram, which ordered local Soviets to prevent any further movement of the Czechoslovak Army to the east and to shoot every Czechoslovak found on the railway brandishing a weapon. The legionaries interpreted this as a declaration of war.

The Czechoslovaks in Russia thus found themselves in three wars simultaneously: first, as part of the Allied forces battle against the Central Powers in the war, which is known as either the Great War or First World War; second, as Czechoslovak troops fighting both against Czech and Slovak loyalists, loyal to Emperor Charles I, and against the Czechoslovak Communists, loyal to Lenin, in the War of Independence of the Czechoslovak Republic in Austria-Hungary and the Soviet Union; and, third, they also became one of many combatants involved in the Russian Civil War.

At the moment of Bolshevik attack the Czechoslovak Corps was stretched along the Trans-Siberian Railway, torn into six isolated groups around several important towns: Penza, Chelyabinsk, Novonikolayevsk, Mariinsk, Nizhn-yeudinsk and Vladivostok. Soldiers from individual groups resisted attempts by the Bolsheviks to disband their units, occupied railway stations where they were located, armed themselves in captured warehouses, and made attempts to connect with other groups.

for the country. Inactivity at railway stations, through which passed freed prisoners, led to a serious incident on 14th May 1918 in Chelyabinsk. In this incident Austro-Hungarian soldiers threw a piece of iron from the train at the Czechoslovaks on the ground as a result a soldier of the 6th Czechoslovak Rifle Regiment was severely wounded. The Czechoslovaks present found the culprit and beat him to death. Local Soviet soldiers arrested members of a Czechoslovak sentry who voluntarily and without weapons came into the Soviet building to give evidence to the

investigation into the incident. The 3rd and 6th Czechoslovak Rifle Regiments seized Chelyabinsk and freed prisoners on 17th May 1918. The conflict with the Soviet government was settled amicably. However, on 21st May, Czechoslovak legionaries received a telegram from the People's Commissar of Defense, Leon Trotsky, who decided to disband all Czechoslovak units. According to this order, they were either to be subsumed into the Red Army or would be transformed into working units. An interim executive committee decided that Czechoslovak troops must depart

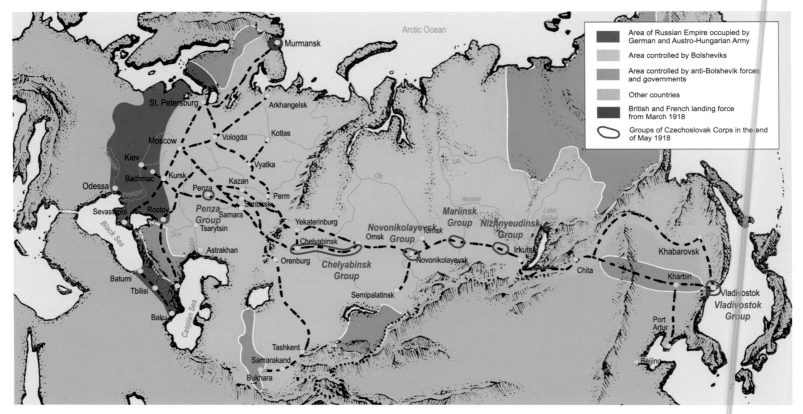

The distribution of Czechoslovak transportation on the Trans-Siberian Railway at the outbreak of hostilities with the Bolsheviks. *Hana Rozmanitá, courtesy of ČSOL*

On 1st June 1918, the Mariinsk and Novonikolayevsk Groups came together to form the Siberian Group. Eight days later, on 9th June, soldiers from the Siberian Group made contact with the Chelyabinsk Group. On this day the Chelyabinsk Group split into the Western and Northwestern Groups, and the Siberian Group was re-named the Eastern Group. On 20th June, after being released from Bolshevik encirclement, units from the Novonikolayevsk Group were absorbed into the Eastern Group, which advanced further east, to Lake Baikal, to connect with the group in Vladivostok. In the west, after several tough battles, the Penza Group managed to connect with the Western group, on 6th July. Two days later, on 8th July, the Western and Northwestern Groups were amalgamated into the Ural Group, which was later re-named after the seizure of Yekaterinburg to the Yekaterinburg Group, on 25th July 1918.

Three Czechoslovak Groups made use of armored cars: Penza Group, Chelyabinsk Group (including Groups that were later formed by its split or renaming), and the Eastern Group.

Garford armored car, GROZNIY (in Russian, "Terrible"), captured the by the 1st Czechoslovak Rifle Regiment in Penza, Russia, on 28th May 1918. The man in a peaked cap standing on a railroad car with his hand under the turret gun is Vladimir Kučka. *Courtesy of VÚA-VHA*

PENZA GROUP

All Czechoslovak trains west of the Volga River were in this group. It consisted of a unit from the 1st Rifle Regiment of Master Jan Hus, 4th Rifle Regiment of Prokop Holý, 1st Hussite reserve battalion, and several batteries of the 1st Artillery Brigade of Jan Žižka. Unlike other Groups, Czechoslovak soldiers from these units were still partially armed.

On the morning of 28th May 1918, soldiers from the 5th Company of 2nd Battalion 1st Regiment captured three armored vehicles at the station in Penza, which were originally intended as reinforcement for the local Soviet: a heavy armored Garford car named GROZNIY (ГРОЗНЫЙ), an Armstrong-Whitworth-Fiat armored car, and a unique single-turreted armored car consisting of parts of Austin armored cars, first and second series, marked only with "kornilovtsi emblem" (a skull and crossbones). In requisitioning these vehicles Czechoslovak soldiers met with little resistance.

On the evening of 28th May, the captured Armstrong-Whitworth-Fiat armored car was mounted onto a flatcar, and used in the second attempt to seize station Penza I. The attack

Armstrong-Whitworth-Fiat, captured in Penza, 28th May 1918. *Courtesy of VHÚ*

Armored train GROZNIY of the 4th Czechoslovak Rifle Regiment in Serdobsk, 29th May 1918. Third from the left is Ensign Sazima, and Vladimir Kučka is sixth from the right. *Courtesy of VÚA-VHA*

View of the city of Penza in Tambov province, Russia 1918. *Courtesy of VÚA-VHA*

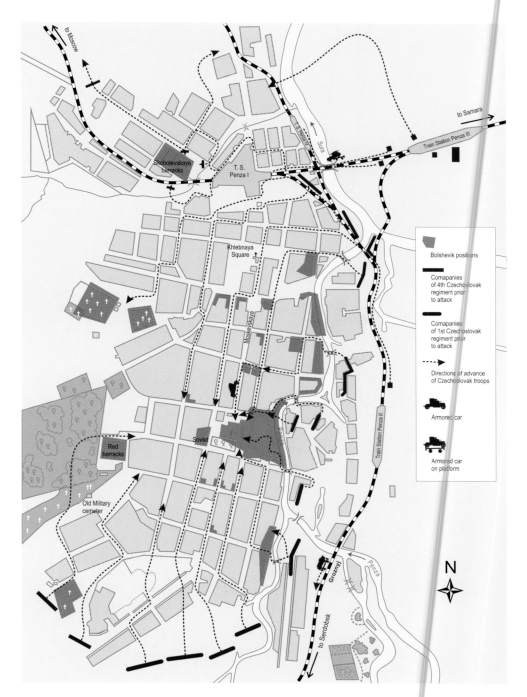

Fight for Penza 29th May 1918. *Hana Rozmanitá, courtesy of ČSOL*

Alexandrovskiy Bridge across the Volga River. *Courtesy of VÚA-VHA*

was refuted, and during the retreat a locomotive with an armored car was derailed on the railway bridge, where it was left. One day later, on 29 May, the 1st and the 4th Czechoslovak Rifle Regiment captured Penza, dispersed the local Soviet garrison (including about two hundred men from the Czechoslovak Communist Regiment), and seized stocks of arms and ammunition, which had been left in Penza by previously disarmed Czechoslovak units. Lieutenant Jiří Švec, who commanded the attack on Penza, fielded, the day before, captured armored cars as well.

A single-turreted Austin, assigned to the 4th Regiment, proceeded with the 9th Company on the right (northern) flank, on Moscow Street. Initially the car had problems with its engine and the crew was unable to negotiate the steep street. The machine even began to spontaneously move backwards, and an attempt by infantrymen to push the car forward was unsuccessful. But soon its engine started and by about eleven o'clock the armored car drove into the square, which at that time was the last bastion of Red resistance. The gunners in the vehicle silenced Bolshevik machine guns on the tower of the church, in the building of local Gubernian Soviet, and in barracks. This success led to the complete seizure of the town by Czechoslovaks.

In his novel *The Great Dream* Rudolf Medek writes that an armored car called GROZNIY was engaged in a battle on Moscow Street and on the main Square in Penza. This is, however, literary fiction. In fact, Garford GROZNIY was located on a flat-car and incorporated into the 4th Czechoslovak Rifle Regiment armored train, called GROZNIY (in which it was the only armored element), on 29th May 1918 at 6 o'clock in the morning. The armored train set out for the southwest, to Serdobsk, to establish a connection with the most westward protruding Czechoslovak unit, the 1st Battalion of the 4th Regiment. The crew of the armored train dispersed forces from

Armored car Armstrong-Whitworth-Fiat of the 1st Czechoslovak Rifle Regiment's armored train ORLÍK, following the collision with an enemy locomotive at Obsharovka station, 31st May 1918. *Courtesy of Jiří Charfreitag*

This is how the armored car Austin first/second series survived an accident. The "Adam's head"— skull and crossbones – symbol of Russian "battalions of death" on the left-hand side of its turret is clearly visible. The motif was preserved even after the Bolsheviks had made use of the vehicle, and it was in this state that it was captured by soldiers of the 1st Czechoslovak Rifle Regiment in Penza, 28th May 1918. *Courtesy of Jiří Charfreitag*

the Serdobsk Soviet, conquered Serdobsk, encountered a Bolshevik train, and allowed the 1st Battalion of the 4th Regiment to reach safety. Until the end of its career Garford GROZNIY served in the Czechoslovak Army on flatcars as a gun wagon of armored trains.

On the evening of 29 May 1918, a single-turreted Austin with a Kornilov sign and an Armstrong-Whitworth-Fiat were placed on platform wagons. Together they came to form the first appearance of armored train of the 1st Regiment, which soon acquired the name ORLÍK. For soldiers belonging to the Penza Group this was an important prerequisite in capturing the Alexandrovsky Bridge across the Volga River, east of Syzran. After midnight on 31st May, the Czechoslovaks reached the bridge, and after 8 o'clock in the morning, after a two-hour battle in which ORLÍK decisively intervened, the one-and-a-half-kilometer long bridge was in Czechoslovak hands. ORLÍK chased a fleeing enemy up to the Obsharovka station, six kilometers from the bridge, where the Bolsheviks unleashed their own "mad" unmanned locomotive. As a result of the ensuing collision the Armstrong-Whitworth-Fiat armored car was completely destroyed and the single-turreted Austin was heavily damaged. Whereas the first vehicle was written off after a three-day servicing by the Czechoslovak Army, the single-turreted Austin was later repaired and served until 1920, initially on flatcars as an improvised armored train car, and later in its original role on the ground.

Czechoslovak trains in the hands of the Penza group progressed down the Trans-Siberian Railway further east, headed by ORLÍK and backed by the GROZNIY armored train. When capturing Obsharovka, on 31st May, the Czechoslovaks clashed with a Bolshevik armored car of an unknown type armed with two machine guns. They clashed once again with the same vehicle on 1st June in an attack on Bezenchuk where soldiers of the 4th Regiment eventually captured it. Legionaries deployed probably the same armored car "with two guns" on 2nd June in a reconnaissance around Ivashchenkovo; and on 4th June 1918, under the command of the deputy officer Brázda, it was also probably sent into battle at Lipyagi. However, two kilometers south of the village of Voskresenskoye the armored vehicle broke down and it did not reach the battlefield. However, in this battle the Czechoslovaks captured two more damaged armored cars: one Fiat-Izhorski with the number 36 on its side, found lying upside down in a ditch, and another Armstrong-

1st Czechoslovak Rifle Regiment's armored train ORLÍK, reconstructed after a collision at Obsharovka. *Courtesy of VÚA-VHA*

Whitworth-Fiat without any markings. This second vehicle remained in the service of Czechoslovak Legions until 1920 as well.

To the rear of the Penza Group Moscow sent its best forces, of about 4,000 men, mostly Germans, Hungarians and Latvians, armed with artillery and three armored cars of an unknown type, probably from the 18th "Flying" Red Army Armored Section. This punitive expedition clashed with the Czechoslovak rear guard on 5th June, in the Second Battle of Bezenchuk. One armored car was chasing the left flank of the Czechoslovak defense line, while the other two maneuvered by the railway line near the Bolshevik armored train. After a day of fighting, less than six companies from the 1st Reserve Regiment and the 1st Rifle Regiment, supported by the GROZNIY armored train, managed not only to stop the Red Army soldiers but also to scare them off altogether, and they retreated. At the station the Czechoslovaks captured one of the Bolshevik armored cars, which had fallen from the railcar whilst being loaded.

The Penza Group captured Samara on 8th June 1918, where the Czechoslovaks received a warm welcome from the local population. In the city the Russian democratic government (KOMUCh, Komitet chlenov uchreditelnogo sobraniya, Committee of Members of the Constituent Assembly) was established, and the anti-Bolshevik Russian People's Army (Narodnaya Armiya) began to form. The Czechoslovaks acquired a secure base there, protected by the Volga River from the west, from where they could fight their way further east to connect with the Chelyabinsk Group. In connecting with units of the Penza Group armored cars played their role once again at the end of June. When conquering Buzuluk from 24th to 26th June 1918, the Czechoslovaks clashed with several armored cars. A turning point in the battle came when the fuel tank of an unknown Bolshevik car was penetrated; and the city fell into Czechoslovak hands on 26th June. Among the spoils was the armored car Fiat-Izhorski, albeit without a motor.

Single-turreted armored car Austin first/second series, serving on a flat car as a machine gun wagon of the 1st Czechoslovak Rifle Regiment's armored train ORLÍK, 2nd June 1918. *Courtesy of VÚA-VHA*

Improvised gun wagon of the ORLÍK armored train before an encounter at Lipyagi. Single turreted Austin is visible on the far left. *Courtesy of VÚA-VHA*

CZECHOSLOVAK ARMORED CARS IN WORLD WAR I AND THE RUSSIAN CIVIL WAR

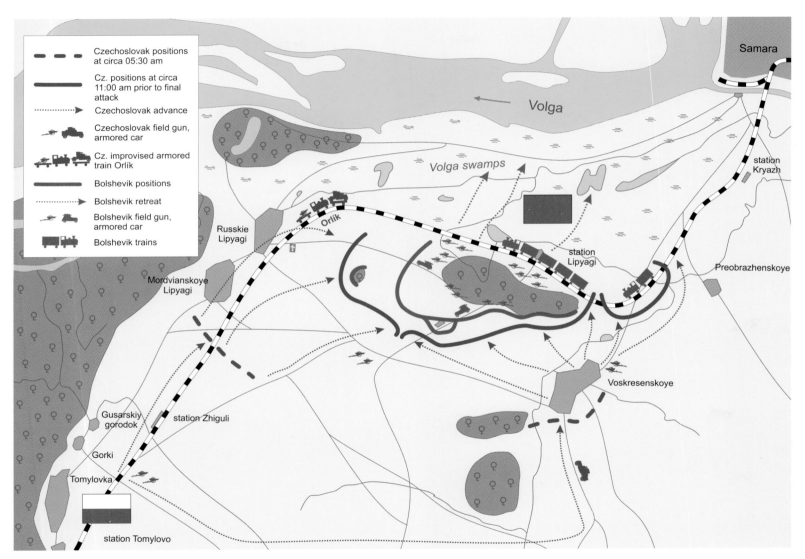

The Battle of Lipyagi, 4th June 1918. *Courtesy of Hana Rozmanitá via ČSOL*

Legend:

- ▬ ▬ ▬ Czechoslovak positions at circa 05:30 am
- ▬▬▬ Cz. positions at circa 11:00 am prior to final attack
- ·······► Czechoslovak advance
- Czechoslovak field gun, armored car
- Cz. improvised armored train Orlík
- ▬▬▬ Bolshevik positions
- ·······► Bolshevik retreat
- Bolshevik field gun, armored car
- Bolshevik trains

Samara

Volga

station Kryazh

Volga swamps

Orlík

Russkie Lipyagi

Mordvianskoye Lipyagi

station Lipyagi

Preobrazhenskoye

Voskresenskoye

Gusarskiy gorodok

station Zhiguli

Gorki

Tomylovka

station Tomylovo

Czechoslovak 4th heavy battery at the Battle of Lipyagi. *Courtesy of VÚA-VHA*

View across battlefield at Lipyagi from the south, in the direction of the Czechoslovak attack. Buildings on the horizon were occupied by the Bolsheviks and armed with a number of machine guns. It was here that the commander of the 4th Czechoslovak Rifle Regiment, Jan Gayer, was mortally wounded. *Courtesy of VÚA-VHA*

Bolsheviks armored car Fiat-Izhorski with the number 36 on its side, captured in the battle at Lipyagi, 4th June 1918. It was camouflaged with a single color, probably green. The small number 36 on its side was painted in white. *Courtesy of VÚA-VHA*

Armored car Armstrong-Whitworth-Fiat, captured at Lipyagi, 4th June 1918. In the foreground are standing volunteers, Kučka, Sergeant Volas, and Lieutenant Jíša. *Courtesy of VÚA-VHA*

Relaxation after the battle at Lipyagi. *Courtesy of VÚA-VHA*

Armstrong-Whitworth-Fiat, captured at Lipyagi, placed on a flatcar. *Courtesy of VÚA-VHA*

Railway station building at Lipyagi. *Courtesy of VÚA-VHA*

Makeshift memorial on the spot where Jan Gayer, the commander of the 4th Czechoslovak Rifle Regiment, was mortally wounded. *Courtesy of VÚA-VHA*

The consequences of fighting in Samara, Russia. *Courtesy of VÚA-VHA*

On 6th July 1918, at the station of Minyar, soldiers from the Penza Group came into contact with soldiers from the Chelyabinsk group, which advanced to meet them from the Urals. The Czechoslovaks decided to stay on the Volga and continue the fight against the Central Powers. This decision was backed by requests from a delegation of liberated Russians. It was also justified on the basis of the ease with which the Czechoslovaks had defeated Bolshevik troops and also by the fact that most Bolshevik units which they faced consisted of Germans, Austrians, and Hungarians hired by the Bolsheviks from POW camps. Some allied officers also encouraged the Czechoslovaks with vague promises of the imminent arrival of Allied troops. The headquarters and remaining regiments of the 1st Czechoslovak Hussite Rifle Division

The welcoming of Czechoslovak troops in Samara, Russia. *Courtesy of VÚA-VHA*

returned to Samara, which became the center of the Volga front, and together with the Russian People's Army it started to purge the western bank of the Volga River from the Bolsheviks.

On 8th July 1918, the Bolsheviks seized Syzran once again. In support of one Czechoslovak company, two battalions of the People's Army, and over 10,000 civilian inhabitants from the city, the 1st and the 3rd battalion of the 4th Rifle Regiment arrived with the armored GROZNIY train, commanded by Lieutenant Pilař. On the night of the 9th-10th July the Czechoslovak-Russian group, under the command of the Russian Colonel Kappel, bypassed the city, and in the morning, the Czechoslovaks and Russians, under the command of Staff Captain Pilař, took back Syzran. On 18th July, armored GROZNIY train carried out an assault ride on Inza. From 1st July the following

operated on the Inza front: the armored train No. 29, under the command of Warrant Officer 1st Class Šrámek, the armored GROZNIY train under lance corporal Dostál, a reserve train of Warrant Officer 1st Class Petřík, trains of the 9th and the 10th Company of the 4th Regiment, a train for cavalry reconnaissance of Sergeant Pleský, and a heavy artillery train of the People's Army. The front was stabilized west of the Bezvodovka station. Up to 20th September there were little substantial changes.

The fate of the Volga front was due to the decisive battles on its flanks. On the Nikolayevsk front on the east bank of the Volga, south of Samara, the use of armored vehicles is not reported. The situation on the northern flank was different, however.

After securing the Syzran beachhead, the 1st Rifle Regiment along with the Russian People's Army began advance on Simbirsk. After securing the station in the village of Bryandino the 1st Rifle Regiment seized an armored car of an unknown

Czechoslovak soldiers in Samara. *Courtesy of VÚA-VHA*

View of Samara, Russia in 1918. *Courtesy of VÚA-VHA*

Armstrong-Whithworth-Fiat armored car in front of the train station in Samara. *Courtesy of VÚA-VHA*

Fiat-Izhorski armored car, captured by the Czechoslovak Legions. *Courtesy of VÚA-VHA*

The crew of the 4th Czechoslovak Rifle Regiment's armored train in Samara, Russia 11th June 1918. *Courtesy of VÚA-VHA*

Cars and lorries captured at Buzuluk, 26 June 1918. In the center lies a Fiat-Izhorski armored car without its engine. *Courtesy of VÚA-VHA*

type named VENOMOUS on 19th July. It is likely that this vehicle was from the British Locker-Lampson's Russian Armoured Car Division RNAS, which was deployed on the Eastern Front on the Russian side since 1916 alongside the Belgian ACM. After the October Revolution it left Russia, leaving there all its vehicles. But by all accounts only three armored cars of the British armored car unit bore the following names: ULSTER, LONDONDERRY and MOUNTJOY. How it came to be that in the summer of 1918 an armored car with an English name appeared in the heart of Russia remains a mystery.

Another armored car of an unknown type left the fleeing Bolsheviks in the village of Bryandino a day later, on 20th July. After the conquest of Simbirsk, on 22nd July, the 1st and the 4th Regiment captured an armored train, "No. 4," under the command of the anarchist Polupanov. It consisted of two gun wagons and an armored engine of Russian Khunkhuz type with attached Russian two-turreted armored rail-cruiser Zaamurets. These modern armored cars became the most famous feature of the ORLÍK armored train.

Armored Cars of the 1st Czechoslovak Rifle Regiment. Fiat-Izhorski on the left, Austin third series on the right. On the basis of the uniforms this picture can be dated to 1918. *Courtesy of VÚA-VHA*

War booty of the 1st and 4th Czechoslovak Rifle Regiments following the seizure of Simbirsk, 22 July 1918. Armored Train "No 4" of the anarchist Polupanov, whose modern armored wagons later became the most famous line-up of the ORLÍK armored train. *Courtesy of VÚA-VHA*

Armored locomotive originally bore the inscription in Cyrillic "Perviy Leninskiy Bronyepoyezd" (The First Leninian Armored Train). *Courtesy of Jiří Charfreitag*

View of a captured armored train on a bridge. *Courtesy of Jiří Charfreitag*

Captured snapshot of the crew of the Bolshevik armored train. The man with binoculars in the middle is probably the anarchist Polupanov. *Courtesy of VÚA-VHA*

The armored train captured in Simbirsk was named ORLÍK. *Courtesy of Jiří Charfreitag*

During an advance on Kazan the 1st Czechoslovak Rifle Regiment clashed with two Bolshevik armored cars probably from the 2nd Machine Armored Automobile Section (2 bronyeviy avtomobilniy otryad) under the command of Commissar Sidorov. This unit had two armored cars of an unknown type. According to the Red Army log from 1st September 1918, the unit was "broken before Kazan." On 1st August 1918 at the Kashinka station, as a result of the efforts of the 1st Czechoslovak Rifle Regiment, both vehicles started to retreat. On 6th August in the port of Kazan one was destroyed and one was captured. One day later, on 7th August 1918, as a result of the combined efforts of Czechoslovak, Russian and Serbian soldiers, Kazan was freed from the Bolsheviks.

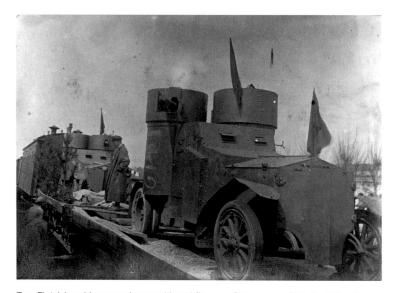

Two Fiat-Izhorski armored cars with red flags on flat wagons. This is all that is known about this picture. In an album belonging to a former member of the 6th Czechoslovak Rifle Regiment, this picture has been preserved with the label "Petropavlovsk, armored cars captured by the Czechoslovak legions." In the estate of another legionary this photo is described as showing captured Bolshevik armored cars at the station in Barabinsk. In the Russian book *Bronyeavtomobili russkoy Armii* it is described as Fiat-Izhorski ACs prior to transportation to the Eastern Front in 1918, and in the Japanese publication *The Photographic Album of the Troubles in Siberia*, published in Tokyo in 1918, these are described as "armored cars, captured by the Japanese Army." However, in the Japanese publication, this photo is placed beside other pictures of Czechoslovak Legions. It is likely that this is probably really Czechoslovak war booty from Petropavlovsk, which the Czechoslovak legions captured on 31st May 1918. *Courtesy of VHÚ*

THE CHELYABINSK GROUP

This group consisted of Czechoslovak trains strewn between Zlatoust and Omsk, which carried the 2nd Czechoslovak Rifle Regiment of Jiří z Poděbrad, the 3rd Czechoslovak Rifle Regiment of Jan Žižka, part of the 6th Czechoslovak Rifle Regiment Hanácký, the HQ of the 1st Czechoslovak Rifle Regiment and the HQ and rear units of the Czechoslovak Corps.

In the advance on Omsk, in the second fight at Maryanovka, on 6th June 1918, the 2nd and 6th Regiment clashed with other Bolshevik units. An armored car was seized that same evening, after the expulsion of the Bolsheviks from the station. It was a unique armored car, a Benz, manufactured by a German company in 1912, by order of the Russian Amur Railway. Its task was to defend the track against bandits, and it had the ability to ride both on the track and on the road. The Chelyabinsk Group conquered Omsk together with Russian Cossacks on 7th June 1918, and, on 9th June 1918, in the Tatarskaya station it seized another armored car of an unknown type. Four days later, on 13th June, a group of 700 men from the 3rd Regiment, again together with Cossacks, attacked Troitsk. It turned out

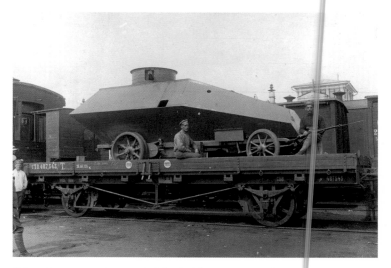

Unique Benz armored car, part of the 2nd Czechoslovak Rifle Regiment's armored train in Omsk, 7th June 1918. *Courtesy of VÚA-VHA*

The 2nd Czechoslovak Rifle Regiment's armored train. *Courtesy of VÚA-VHA*

General Jan Syrový (second from right) and Captain Hess (first from right) with other officers surrounding the Benz armored car in Chelyabinsk. Note the square hole with rounded corners in the rear lower side of the vehicle, which shines through the porthole on the right hand side. *Courtesy of VÚA-VHA*

The armored Benz car also served as part of an armored train on the Ural front. On the roof of the turret is a two-piece open hatch. *Courtesy of VÚA-VHA*

Benz armored car in Czechoslovak armored train on the Urals Front. The inscription on the rear side is URALŠTÍ DIVOŠI (Wild Men From the Ural Mountains). *Courtesy of VÚA-VHA*

Cossack cavalry. *Courtesy of VÚA-VHA*

A Fiat-Izhorski armored car captured by Czechoslovak soldiers in Troitsk. *Courtesy of VÚA-VHA*

Dealing with captured cars in Troitsk, 17th June 1918. On the right can be seen an armored Fiat-Izhorski car. *Courtesy of VHÚ*

The same scene a few minutes later: second from the right is colonel (later general) Voytsekhovski. *Courtesy of VHÚ*

On Saturday 29th June 1918, the 3rd Battalion of the 2nd Regiment seized the Zlokazovo station. One day later, Czechoslovak soldiers faced a counterattack of a Bolshevik armored train, which contained a Garford armored car VITYAZ (ВИТЯЗЬ) on a flatcar. Lieutenant Netík hit the enemy train with his gun from a flatcar of the Czechoslovak improvised armored train, which caused internal explosion of ammunition in Garford and resulted in the retreat of the Bolshevik armored train.

After the decision not to leave Russia, and instead to create a new front against the Central Powers, the Chelyabinsk Group proceeded towards Yekaterinburg before dividing into the West and Northwest Groups. During the attack on the Vagay station, on the morning of 4th July, the 6th Regiment faced a counterattack from a Bolshevik armored car, a Fiat-Izhorski. But the armored car was soon repulsed by the troops.

On 22nd July, after the capture of Khrompik by units of the 3rd Regiment, Czechoslovak troops of the 3rd Shock Company approached a Bolshevik armored car Austin 2nd series, whose driver mistakenly took them to be a skirmish line of his own troops. When the crew of the car discovered their mistake, they started randomly shooting around. Shock troopers, under the command of Captain Žák, knocked out the machine gunner in the right turret. Captain Žák then blocked the machine gun in the turret with his bayonet so that the vehicle crew could not resume active fire. Other shock troopers then threw a grenade into the

that the Bolshevik garrison in the city was stronger than expected. Bolshevik armored cars patrolling the streets counterattacked, and one managed to penetrate the rear of Czechoslovaks forces. Its machine-guns soon stopped working fortunately, and the armored car retreated. The Czechoslovak and Russian forces withdrew as well. The second attack at Troitsk on 16th June took almost the entire 3rd Regiment, along with parts of the 2nd Regiment, the 3rd Shock Company and other support troops, including both armored cars captured on the previous day. In the evening a pincer group gathered, consisting of the 3rd Shock Company, the 1st Battalion of the 3rd Regiment, and a machine gun section and about 20

cavalrymen. They passed the Bolshevik position from the west and on the morning on the 17th June attacked Troitsk via the Moslem cemetery. From the north they simultaneously attacked both frontal groups–one on the left and one to the right of the track, each supported by armored cars. However, the vehicles experienced problems advancing over the sandy terrain and became bogged down. The pincer group at the Mohammedan cemetery clashed with a Bolshevik armored car and with two others in a street fight in the town. Shock-troopers knocked out one of them with hand grenades. In total, Czechoslovaks of Troitsk captured three armored cars after the conquest, one of them Fiat-Izhorski.

A Bolshevik armored car, Austin second series, destroyed by Czechoslovak soldiers of the 3rd Shock Company in Khrompik, 23rd July 1918. The entire vehicle was camouflaged by a single color, probably green. The white-blue-red cockades were painted on the side of the turret and on the side of the driver. *Courtesy of VÚA-VHA*

The same car, view from the back. *Courtesy of VÚA-VHA*

Austin wreckage besieged by Khrompik residents. *Courtesy of VÚA-VHA*

Captain Žák, wounded in the battle at Khrompik, with his officers. *Courtesy of VÚA-VHA*

Czechoslovak military band plays at the railway station for local Khrompik residents. *Courtesy of VÚA-VHA*

Bolshevik armored car, a Fiat-Izhorski, set ablaze by soldiers of the 6th Czechoslovak Rifle Regiment at Vagay station, 4th July 1918 in the morning. *Courtesy of Jiří Cahrfreitag*

vehicle through a loophole on the left-hand side, which set the vehicle on fire. Its entire crew perished.

After the capture of Yekaterinburg, on 25 July 1918, the city became the base of the Ural front and the HQ of the 2nd Czechoslovak Rifle Division. On 3rd August Czechoslovak armored cars helped to secure the city from attack from the north. On the morning of 6th August the 6th Czechoslovak Rifle Regiment seized Sarga station on the Permian Railway track at the Kungur front. According to a picture from the regiment's history, the regiment captured an armored car, Jeffery-Poplavko, which was loaded on a flatcar. On 7th August the Yekaterinburg defense commander, Warrant Officer 1st Class Číla, sent one armored car and a company of Bashkirs as reinforcements to Krasnoufimsk,

west of the city. One day later, on the order of General Voytsekhovsky, Warrant Officer 1st Class Číla sent one armored car to strengthen the attack on Baltyk and Mostovskaya. The same day, 8th August, the 2nd Czechoslovak Rifle Regiment put one armored car into field at Pyshmy, northeast of Yekaterinburg. The fight continued on 9th August too. The Czechoslovak armored car became bogged down in the sand and the Bolsheviks suffered great losses

in an attempt to seize it. Between 8th and 13th August, the 2nd Regiment captured an armored car in the village of Baltym. One Bolshevik armored car operated on 10th September before the newly built Russian Irkutsk Division, that replaced the Czechoslovaks in the Krasnoufimsk direction. In the next advance on Perm and central Ural armored cars are not mentioned.

The Bolshevik armored car, destroyed at Vagay station. On its left-hand side it carried an inscription in Cyrillic—"RABOCHIY" i.e. "worker." *Courtesy of Jiří Cahrfreitag*

View of Yekaterinburg, Russia in 1918. *Courtesy of VÚA-VHA*

Czechoslovak war booty also included Holt tracked tractors. *Courtesy of VÚA-VHA*

Armored car, Jeffery-Poplavko, captured by the 6th Czechoslovak Rifle Regiment at Sarga station on the Kungur railway, 6th August 1918. *Courtesy of VÚA-VHA*

JAN NETÍK

Jan Netík was born on 12th November 1885 in the village of Roveň in the Rychnov nad Kněžnou district of Bohemia. After graduating from a school in Rychnov, he enrolled for service in the Austro-Hungarian Army. In 1911 he successfully graduated from the Faculty of Arts of Charles University and pursued a career as a gymnasium teacher. In August 1914 he was called up to the Austro-Hungarian 3rd Fortress Artillery Regiment on the Eastern front, where in March 1915 he was captured. In a POW camp situated in Ufa in June 1916 he joined the Czechoslovak Legion, and in July of the same year he was assigned to reserve units of the Czechoslovak Rifle Brigade. After a year of service he became an officer, and for two months commanded the 3rd company of the 8th Czechoslovak Rifle Regiment, before being assigned to the artillery. First, he served in the artillery section of the 5th Czechoslovak Rifle Regiment, from September 1917, and in the 2nd Independent Artillery Section. In the early phase of the conflict with the Bolsheviks he was a deputy to the first congress of the Czechoslovak Army in Russia. In several skirmishes with the Bolsheviks he was a battery commander in the Chelyabinsk Group. He was wounded in a fight at the Zlokazovo station on 30th June 1918. After recovering, in August 1918 he became a battery commander in the 2nd Czechoslovak Artillery Brigade. In 1919 he successively commanded the 2nd and then also, from April 1919, the 3rd Independent Heavy Artillery Section.

He returned home on 22nd July 1920. In September 1920 he was appointed commander of the Medium Artillery Regiment 108 in Hlučín. In May 1922 he was called to the artillery division of the Ministry of National Defence (MNO). On 5th September 1925 he became commander of the 1st Field Artillery Brigade. Three years later, in May 1928, he achieved the rank of General and returned to the MNO, where in January 1929 he became head of the 2nd department (Artillery and Arming). He held this post until the German Occupation.

At the time of mobilization in September 1938, General Netík served as a commander of the artillery headquarters in the Račice Castle at Vyškov. At the turn of 1938/1939 he dealt with other Czechoslovak generals and high officers to discuss the possibilities of further developments in the military situation at that time. These consultations resulted in the creation of a military resistance organization, Obrana Národa (ON, Defense of the Nation). After the occupation of the remainder of Czechoslovakia, in March 1939, Netík was appointed a representative of General Eliáš during the liquidation of the Ministry of National Defense. His task was to place former Czechoslovak officers in the civilian industry according the needs of the ON. For participation in the home resistance movement and providing assistance to the Czechoslovak resistance in exile, he was arrested on 30th September 1939. He died on 17th February 1945 in the Buchenwald concentration camp.

Ranks: Austro-Hugarian Army: 2nd October 1905 One Year Volunteer, 1st January 1907 Cadet. Czechoslovak Army: July 1917 Lieutenant, 13th September 1918 Sub-Captain, 21st December 1918 Major, 1919 Lieutenant Colonel, 1st December 1922 Colonel of Artillery, 1st May 1928 Brigadier General, 30th December 1929 Major General.

Decorations and awards include: Russian Order of St. Anne's third degree with swords and ribbon, Czechoslovak order Sokol first degree with swords and ribbon, French War Cross with palm, the order of the Romanian Crown, Order of the Yugoslav Crown and many others. 27th July 1926 Knights Cross of the French Legion of Honour.

Jan Netík on the left (later general).
Courtesy of VÚA-VHA

Colonel Gajda enters Irkutsk leading his troops on 28th July 1918. *Courtesy of VÚA-VHA*

EASTERN GROUP

The Eastern group included the Shock Battalion (without the 3rd Shock Company), part of the 6th Rifle Regiment Hanácký, the 7th Rifle Regiment Tatra and part of the 2nd Artillery Brigade. When connected to the Nizhneudinsk Group on 20th June 1918 units of the 2nd Reserve Regiment, half of one of companies of the 8th Rifle Regiment Silesian and rear units from the 2nd Rifle Division strengthened it. The same day the Eastern group took up positions east of Nizhneudinsk. Bolshevik units from the Irkutsk Soviet, consisting primarily of German and Hungarian infantry drafted from POW camps, advanced on Nizhneudinsk by rail, covered by an armored train; cavalry and an armored car of an unknown type "with two rotating turrets" advanced to Nizhneudinsk on the Irkutsk road. Early in the morning on 24th June the armored car on the road from Irkutsk undertook a reconnaissance raid on Czechoslovak positions and retreated after a brief firefight. It then stood on

Czechoslovak soldiers enjoy a moment of relaxation on Trapezovskaya Street in Irkutsk. *Courtesy of VÚA-VHA*

The rugged terrain of the coast of Lake Baikal. *Courtesy of VÚA-VHA*

the Irkutsk road, at a distance of about 300 meters. The morning was relatively calm and filled with mutual artillery duels. At noon the armored car started up and began to move in slow motion, which coincided with the Bolshevik attack. An armored car chased the left flank of the Czechoslovak front, occupied by the 10th and the 11th Company of the 7th regiment, and ventured up to fifteen meters to the Czechoslovak positions. But due to the soggy road the car could not get close, and then retreated. However, it turned out that the Czechoslovak defense had no effective weapons to use. At about five o'clock the Bolsheviks repeated their attack and after the armored car penetrated Czechoslovak lines, they occupied frontal Czechoslovak trenches. But that day they did not proceed further and retreated at night. After the start of the Czechoslovak advance towards Irkutsk, on 26 June, no armored car is mentioned. The Eastern Group captured Irkutsk, capital of Eastern Siberia, on 11th July 1918.

From 15th to 20th August 1918 the Eastern Group under the command of Czech Colonel Gajda secured passage around Lake Baikal. In this area the Trans-Siberian Railway leads through extremely rugged terrain with lots of tunnels, and a frontal attack there was out of the question. Therefore, a pincer group under the command of Russian Lieutenant Colonel Ushakov, which consisted of about 1000 men, sailed on the steamboats Buryat, Feodosia and Sibiryak across Lake Baikal, before landing near the village of Posolskaya, at the rear of Bolshevik troops on 16th August 1918. It consisted of the Czech Shock Battalion of Lieutenant Hásek, Russian Barnaul Regiment, the 1st Company of the 7th Czechoslovak Rifle Regiment, a half of the 4th Company of the 8th Rifle Regiment, a Cossack cavalry section, and two Russian and four Czechoslovak guns. When returning from Posolskaya, after the pincer group landed, the Czechoslovak vessels met near the Mysovaya Bolshevik armed icebreaker Baikal, which they managed

Colonel Ushakov departs via the BURYAT steamer to Lake Baikal on 14th August 1918. *Courtesy of VÚA-VHA*

The pincer group aboard the BURYAT steamer (note gun attachments). *Courtesy of VÚA-VHA*

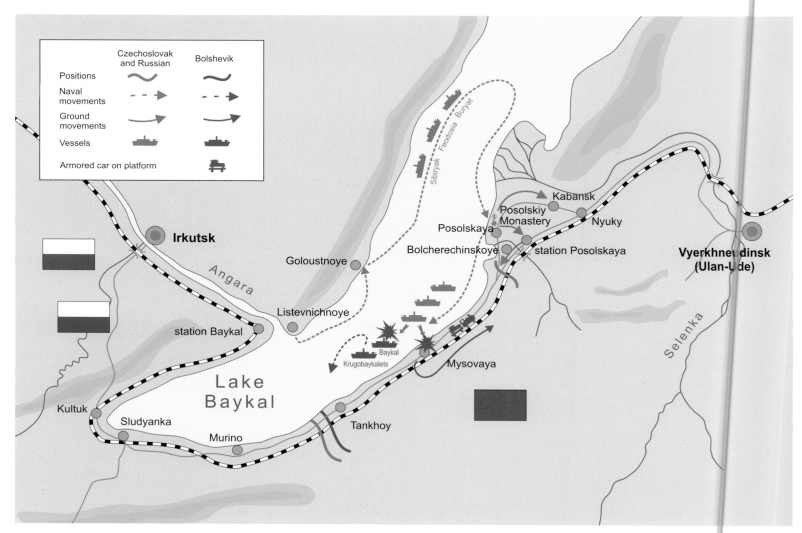

Pincer operation across Lake Baikal, 15th-20th August 1918. *Hana Rozmanitá, courtesy of ČSOL*

to sink. Then they met the Bolshevik-controlled Krugobaykalets steamer, which they damaged. The Czechoslovak ships proceeded to shell fired Bolshevik trains at the Mysovaya station. Around 2,000 Bolshevik troops were concentrated there, and they panicked and fled to the east. At the Posolskaya station they attacked the pincer group. The Bolsheviks managed to pass one armored car out of the flatcar, which was deployed in combat, but the pincer group scattered these Bolshevik units and captured the armored car on 17th August. After hearing the news Soviet troops numbering about 3,000 men began to retreat to the east on 16th August. On the evening of 17th August they arrived at the Posolskaya station. The Barnaul regiment commander retreated under their pressure to the village of Posolskaya, which lies to the north. As a result, the Bolsheviks captured the commander of the pincer group, Colonel Ušakov. The Pincer group units hastily built a defensive line to the west of Posolskaya. The captured armored car (with a broken engine) was placed on the crossing of the vehicle route across the train track but Bolsheviks soon captured it. Much stronger Bolshevik units managed to divide the pincer group into four segments. The units remained split until the arrival of General Gajda's forces on the morning of 18th August. They joined Czechoslovak units at the Posolskaya station, where they captured most of the Bolshevik trains stranding in front of the destroyed railway bridge. On 20th August 1918 the Eastern Group captured

Disembarking of pincer group at Posolskaya Monastery, 16th August 1918. *Courtesy of VÚA-VHA*

Burning railway bridges at Posolskaya station, set ablaze by the pincer group. *Courtesy of VÚA-VHA*

Vyerkhnyeudinsk and continued in the direction of Vladivostok.

In other operations of the Eastern Group armored vehicles are not mentioned. However, in the Karymskaya station an unmarked armored car, a Fiat-Izhorski, was photographed loaded on a flatcar, which is likely to have been the same car as in all the cases mentioned above.

Undated snapshot of a Fiat-Izhorski armored car at Karymskaja station. (However, according to another source, it is nearby Olovyannaya station.) It is likely that this armored car was captured and used by the pincer group at Posolskaya. *Courtesy of VÚA-VHA*

Monument to fallen Czechoslovaks and Russians of the pincer group at Posolskaya, built by the architect V. Kvasnička with sculptures by K. Babka in 1919. There was a common grave of Czechoslovak soldiers on the left and that of Russian soldiers on the right. *Courtesy of VÚA-VHA*

Sketch of the Posolskaya memorial. *Courtesy of VÚA-VHA*

A turret of a captured Fiat-Izhorski armored car, loaded on a wagon, Inza railway. *Courtesy of VÚA-VHA*

AUTUMN AND WINTER 1918 – TRIUMPH AND TRAGEDY

On 31st August 1918, in the Karymskaya station, units of the Eastern Group met with units of the Vladivostok Group. That meant that after three months of fighting, the Trans-Siberian Railway from the Volga to the Pacific Ocean was in Czechoslovak hands. Together with vast spaces of Eastern Russia, the Urals, Siberia, and the Far East as well, this was equivalent to an area twice the size of Europe. But despite territorial gains, the main Czechoslovak success was blocking 500,000 Austrian and Hungarian and another few hundred thousand German prisoners in Russian prison camps in Siberia and Kazakhstan. The number of soldiers, who up to that point avoided slaughter on the western front, totaled up to one million. Together with the arrival of the American Army in France, this was a decisive moment in which the balance of power in the First World War

GROZNIY armored train on the Inza railway. *Courtesy of VÚA-VHA*

The rear side of the Garford GROZNIY gun turret. *Courtesy of VÚA-VHA*

finally turned in favor of the Entente Powers. The enormous achievements of the Czechoslovak Legion also brought international recognition of Czechoslovak independence and the Czechoslovak National Council in Paris as the official Representative of the emerging Czechoslovak state. The performance of the Czechoslovak Legion in Russia both in the First World War and in the War of Independence, was crowned by a complete and resounding success. In the third war in which the Legion found itself, the Russian Civil War, events however took a tragic turn. Russians on liberated territories too slowly realized how deadly danger threatened them from the Bolsheviks and only tentatively built their own volunteer army. The Entente Powers, exhausted by the lasting Great War, sent only limited help to restored Russian democracy. In contrary, Lenin, the psychopathic Bolshevik leader, introduced mandatory conscription to the Red Army, and in full awareness of German neutrality in the west, enticed Soviet forces to rise up against the Russian People's Army and Czechoslovak 1st Rifle Division on the Volga. Kazan fell on 10th September 1918 and the Volga front gradually collapsed under the pressure of Bolshevik forces.

The Garford GROZNIY, under the command of lance corporal Dostál, withdrew from Inza to the Volga along with six other Czechoslovak trains. On 22nd September, in the village of Rachaytse, a Bolshevik pincer section attacked a Czechoslovak reserve and armored train "No. 29" of Warrant

The GROZNIY armored train was a favorite object for group photos, here pictured with Red Cross nurses. *Courtesy of VÚA-VHA*

Left side of the Garford GROZNIY. *Courtesy of VÚA-VHA*

Officer 1st Class Šrámek, who formed the rearguard. An attempt at night to recover the two trains from the area failed and both trains went up in flames after being emptied. During the retreat Russian and Czechoslovak evacuation trains congregated in front of the Alexandrovsky Bridge, whilst armored trains waited at the station in Batraki. GROZNIY arrived at Batraki on 2nd October. The Czechoslovaks kept their positions on the right flank of the western bank of the Volga, whereas Russian soldiers of the People's Army were in the middle, with a battalion of Bashkirs on the left wing. When the Bolsheviks advanced on 3rd October, the Russians immediately withdrew across the bridge. After finding that the center of the position was undefended, the Czechoslovaks managed to retreat as well, but the Bashkirs were cut off and massacred. Witnesses described similar scenes during the Tarnopol retreat of the Russian Army in 1917. On the West Bank there remained three armored trains, and two trains of tanks with diesel fuel, whereas six other trains were cut off altogether. The armored train GROZNIY probably fell into the hands of the Bolsheviks in front of the Alexandrovsky Bridge on 3rd October 1918.

A heavy armored car of an unknown type called GROZNIY was featured among the Armed Forces of General Denikin on 15th September 1919, whose commander was Colonel Barkalov. Because the Russian anti-Bolshevik movement in the south, east and north of the country never established direct contact, this fact has two possible explanations. Either the

Car park of the 1st Czechoslovak Rifle Division HQ. In the background can be seen the following armored cars: Armstrong-Whithworth-Fiat, Austin third series, and a single turreted Austin first/second series. *Courtesy of VÚA-VHA*

Czechoslovak armored cars Austin third series (left) and Armstrong-Whitworth-Fiat (almost invisible in the middle) in the autumn of 1918. *Courtesy of VÚA-VHA*

6th Czechoslovak Rifle Regiment's armored train with turrets from a Fiat-Izhorski armored car. *Courtesy of VÚA-VHA*

Czechoslovak GROZNIY was used by the Red Army, from which soldiers of General Denikin captured it in 1919, or it was a different vehicle, whose crews named it identically.

The single-turreted Austin was deployed in a counterattack at Samara against Bolshevik troops, which invaded from the south on 2nd October. It penetrated the village of Voskresenskoye and Kamenny Brod on the river Mocha, where it managed to scatter the incoming Bolshevik section. Two days later, an Armstrong-Whitworth-Fiat armored car was deployed in the direction of Novonikolayevsk. The Czechoslovaks and Russians completed the evacuation of Samara on 6th October 1918 and retreated to the southern Urals. The loyalty of Czechoslovak soldiers of the 1st Rifle Division, retreating from the Volga, exhausted by combat and demoralized by their experience of Russian society and also by Bolshevik propaganda, began to wane. The crisis peaked in Aksakovo in the early hours of 25th October 1918. After his soldiers expressed their lack of trust, the commander of 1st Hussite Rifle Division, Colonel Josef Jiří Švec, committed suicide. His ultimate act of self-sacrifice restored discipline again.

A day later, in a telegram to the German Emperor Wilhelm II, the Austrian Emperor Karl I wrote "… my nations are no longer able or willing to continue the war," and within 24 hours he requested a separate peace from the Entente Powers, and an immediate truce. On the same day Emperor Wilhelm II released General Ludendorff, the main architect of German aid to the Bolsheviks and

Evacuation of Czechoslovak artillery from Kazan in mid-September 1918. *Courtesy of VÚA-VHA*

in the previous two years in fact, the military dictator of Germany. In Philadelphia, USA, a four-day congress devoted to oppressed central European nations came to an end: Poles, Yugoslavs, Ukrainians, Ruthenians, Lithuanians, Romanians, Italians from Austria, Greeks, Albanians, Jews and Armenians signed a declaration of common objectives on 26th October 1918. Professor T.G Masaryk, as President of this Congress, symbolically rang a replica of the Liberty Bell from 1776 at the end of the event. Two days later, on 28th October 1918, after the publication of Austria's request for armistice, Czechoslovak independence was declared in Prague. The Reuters office in Vladivostok carried news of this event on 2nd November, from where it was reprinted in the Yekaterinburg-based Československý deník, a Czechoslovak daily newspaper, on 5th November.

On the night of 17th-18th November 1918 in Omsk the Warfare Minister of the Russian Government at that time, Vice-Admiral Alexander Kolchak, undertook a military coup. Faced with the collapse of the Volga Front he raised tough government. By using political assassinations and executions of his anti-Bolshevik political rivals he soon began to proficiently imitate his communist opponents. It led to another diversion of democratically minded Czechoslovak Legionnaires from the Russian problems. Czechoslovak regiments, together with the Russians, conquered Perm in the Urals in the last weeks of 1918. By mid-January 1919 they gradually passed over their position to the Russian Army, and withdrew to the rear.

Aerospace and automotive materials evacuated from the Volga front at the end of September 1918, laid out at the Obsharovka station after a train crash. There is a Holt tractor on the right of the picture. *Courtesy of VÚA-VHA*

Evacuation of Samara at the beginning of October 1918. *Courtesy of VÚA-VHA*

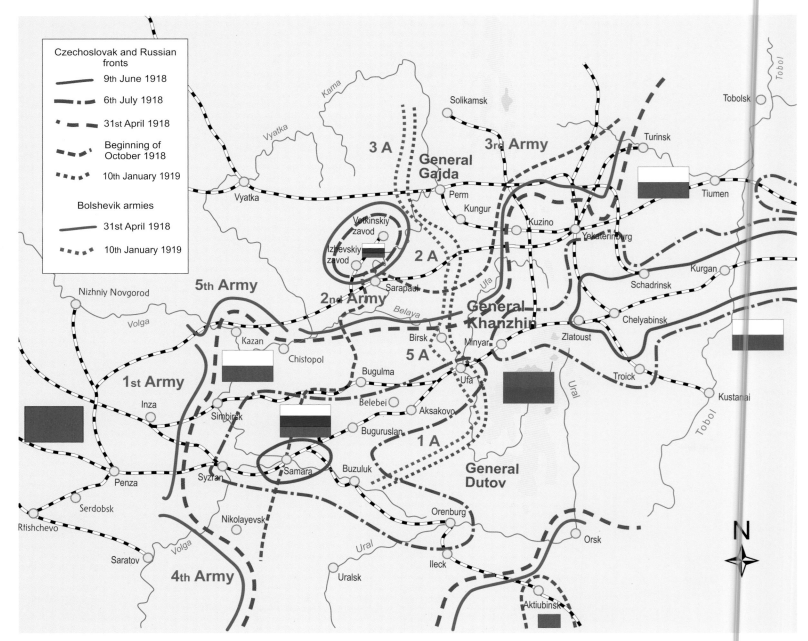

Movements of anti-Bolshevik fronts in the Volga region and the Urals in 1918. *Hana Rozmanitá, courtesy of ČSOL.*

CZECHOSLOVAK ARMORED CARS IN WORLD WAR I AND THE RUSSIAN CIVIL WAR

JOSEF JIŘÍ ŠVEC

Josef Švec was born on 19th July 1883 in Čenkov, in the district of Jihlava. He attended school in Pelhřimov, and later continued his studies at the Teachers' Institute. Starting in 1903 he worked at an elementary school in Třebíč. In 1911 he was sent by the Czech Sokol gymnastic association as a physical education teacher to a girls school in Yekaterinodar in the Caucasus. After the outbreak of the First World War he volunteered for the Czech Druzhina, on 24th August 1914. Between 1914 and 1915 he distinguished himself fighting in the Carpathians and also in Gorlice. In December 1916 during the conversion of a significant proportion of Czechoslovak Brigade soldiers to the Russian Orthodox faith, he also converted and took the name Jiří (George). From 1916 he commanded the 8th company of the 1st Czechoslovak Rifle Regiment, which he also led in the Battle of Zborov. From August 1917 he commanded the 3rd Battalion of the 1st Czechoslovak Rifle Regiment of Master Jan Hus. On 25th February 1918 during the retreat of the Czechoslovak Rifle Corps from Ukraine he became the first Czechoslovak officer ever to coordinate defense against enemy armored fighting vehicles. After the conflict with the Bolsheviks began he assumed command of the 1st Czechoslovak Rifle Regiment. He commanded all Czechoslovak forces in the conquest of Penza. Here again he was the first Czechoslovak officer ever to deploy armored fighting vehicles in combat. He participated in the conquest of Kazan and Samara. And he also oversaw the defense of Kazan and its evacuation. In mid-October 1918 Švec assumed command of the 1st Rifle Division. When his soldiers refused to fulfill their orders to stop the Bolshevik advance on Ufa, he shot himself in the early hours of 25 October 1918. He was buried in Chelyabinsk on 28th October 1918 on the same day when Czechoslovak independence was proclaimed in Prague. In September 1933 his remains were moved to the country, and on 1st October 1933 he was buried for the second time in the Liberation Monument in Prague. In the autumn of 1940, according to Nazi orders, his remains were transferred for the third time to his family's grave in Třešť.

Ranks in Czechoslovak Army: 1st January 1915 Corporal, 5th March 1915 Sergeant, 18th May 1915 Warrant Officer 1st Class, 4th January 1917 First Lieutenant, 4th August 1917 Lieutenant, 27th August 1918 Colonel.

Honors: 23rd July 1915 Russian St. George Medal IV grade, 2nd November 1915 Russian Order of St. Stanislav III degree with swords and ribbon, 3rd June 1916 Russian Order of St. Anna IV degree with an inscription For Bravery, 27th October 1917 Russian St. George Cross IV degree and in 1923 posthumously Czechoslovak Order of M. R. Štéfánik Sokol with swords.

Josef Jiří Švec as an officer of the Czech Druzhina at the front in the Carpathians. From left to right: volunteers Šidlík, Eisenberger, Švec, Podmol and Kouklík. *Courtesy of VÚA-VHA*

Josef Švec (top row, second from left) seen as a professor of physical education at a secondary school in Yekaterinodar, 1912. *Courtesy of VÚA-VHA*

A monument to Colonel Josef Jiří Švec in Prague-Pohořelec was unveiled in 1934, which was designed by the colonel's namesake, the sculptor Otakar Švec. The Nazis removed the statue in 1941. The Restitution Commission of the U.S. Army later found it in Bavaria and returned it to Czechoslovakia after the war, but the Communist regime scrapped it after 1949. The sculptor Otakar Švec won a competition for the design of a memorial to Joseph Stalin in the same year. He took his life in April 1955, a month before the dedication of the monument to Stalin. Stalin's monument in Prague (the biggest in the world) was dismantled by the communists themselves in 1962, following Nikita Khrushchev's famed speech in Moscow about Stalin's cult of personality. *Courtesy of VÚA-VHA*

1919 – TRANS-SIBERIAN RAILWAY PROTECTION

By 1st February 1919 the Czechoslovak Rifle Corps in Russia was reorganized into the Czechoslovak Army in Russia, with three divisions and several other independent units. The Czechoslovaks now assumed guard over the Trans-Siberian Railway to the rear of Kolchak's troops. Czechoslovak units guarded the 20-km-wide corridor along the track from Novonikolayevsk to Kultuk to the east of Irkutsk in central Siberia. In April 1919 they stymied Bolshevik rebellion in Siberia and throughout the year they undertook operations against Bolshevik partisans who tried to disrupt traffic along the railway. Most of the armored cars they captured had already been passed on to the Russian Army in the winter, but a few of them were kept and used in counter-partisan actions. On 24 August 1919 the first Czechoslovak armored unit appeared – the Armored Cars Section, which was supposed to consist one motorcycle, one truck and four armored cars.

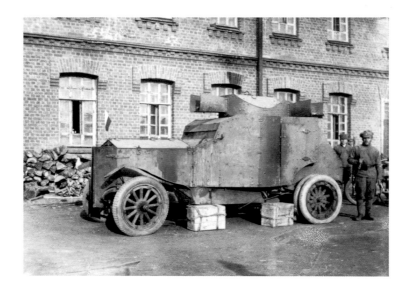

Armstrong-Whithworth-Fiat armored car in Czechoslovak Army barracks at Irkutsk, 1919. *Courtesy of VÚA-VHA and VHÚ.*

Bugler of the 1st Czechoslovak Rifle Regiment in Irkutsk. *Courtesy of VÚA-VHA*

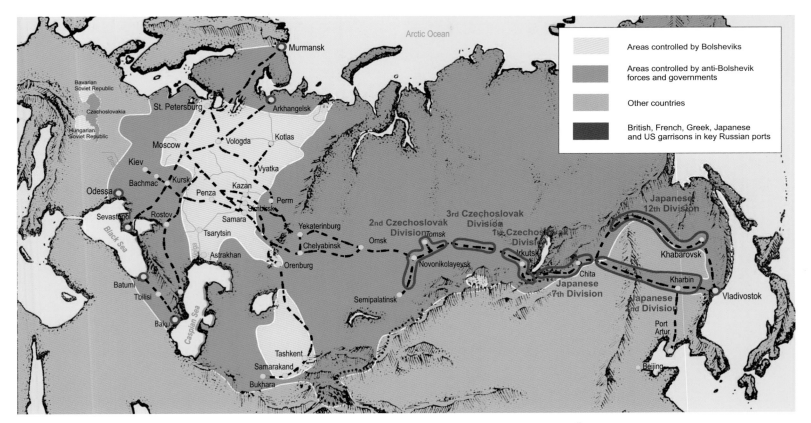

The dislocation of Czechoslovak units down the Trans-Siberian Railway in spring-summer 1919. *Hana Rozmanitá, courtesy of ČSOL*

Map labels:

Arctic Ocean

Bavarian Soviet Republic
Czechoslovakia
Hungarian Soviet Republic
Murmansk
St. Petersburg
Arkhangelsk
Kotlas
Moscow
Vologda
Kiev
Vyatka
Bachmac
Kursk
Kazan
Penza
Perm
Odessa
Simbirsk
Sevastopol
Rostov
Samara
Yekaterinburg
Tsarytsin
Chelyabinsk
Omsk
Astrakhan
Orenburg
Batumi
Tbilisi
Baku
Semipalatinsk
Black Sea
Caspian Sea
Tashkent
Samarakand
Bukhara

2nd Czechoslovak Division
Tomsk
3rd Czechoslovak Division
Novonikolayevsk
1st Czechoslovak Division
Irkutsk
Chita
Japanese 7th Division
Japanese 12th Division
Khabarovsk
Kharbin
Vladivostok
Japanese 2nd Division
Port Artur
Beijing

Legend:
Areas controlled by Bolsheviks
Areas controlled by anti-Bolshevik forces and governments
Other countries
British, French, Greek, Japanese and US garrisons in key Russian ports

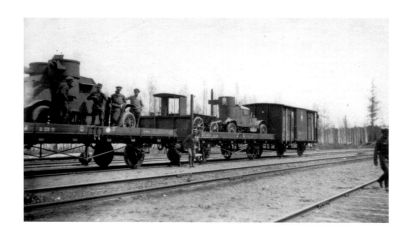

The transportation of ONDRÁŠ and JURÁŠ armored cars at Yurty station before the attack on Kontorskoye. Note JURÁŠ still has the motif skull and crossbones on its turret. *Courtesy of VHÚ*

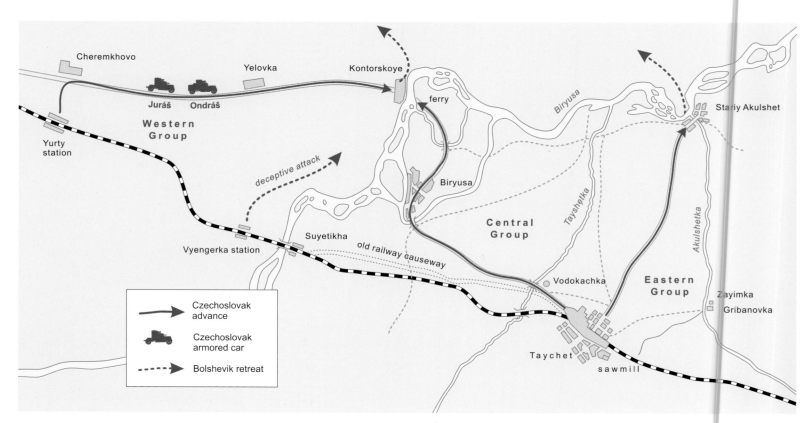

Operations against the Bolsheviks in the village of Kontorskoye. *Hana Rozmanitá, courtesy of ČSOL*

The use of armored vehicles happened for example in late May and June 1919 at Tayshet in an area guarded by the 1st Czechoslovak Division. On 21st May volunteers of the Shock Battalion evicted Bolshevik partisans from the village of Biryusa, on the eastern bank of the river of the same name, near the Trans-Siberian Railway. A guerrilla group numbering approximately 1,000 gunmen then moved to the village of Kontorskoye on the other side of the Biryusa River. In the following days Czechoslovak units in Tayshet were reinforced by two armored cars, an Austin third series ONDRÁŠ and a single-turreted Austin first/second series JURÁŠ.

On 26th May three groups of Czechoslovaks set out from Tayshet. Three armored trains during the operation patrolled the track. The Eastern group, consisting of the 3rd Battalion of the 1st Czechoslovak Rifle Regiment and the 1st Machine Gun Company, forced out Bolshevik guerrillas from the Stary Akulshet. The Western group, composed of units from the 2nd Czechoslovak Rifle Regiment, pretended to attack the Vyengerka station from the north, but its main forces, containing both armored cars, advanced from Yurty station, through Yelovka on Kontorskoye from the west. Captain Pittner commanded the single-turreted Austin during this operation. The Central group, consisting of the Shock Battalion, in addition to machine-guns from the 4th Czechoslovak Rifle Regiment and two guns from the 1st Artillery Regiment,

The advance on the village of Kontorskoye was hindered by a soggy surface in May 1919. In this picture a single turreted Austin first/second series JURÁŠ is seen bogged down in the mud in the village of Yelenskoye. *Courtesy of VÚA-VHA*

Austin third series, ONDRÁŠ, also had problems with the mud in Yelenskoye. *Courtesy of VÚA-VHA*

Rest following the advance and conquest of Kontorskaya. *Courtesy of VÚA-VHA*

Infantry advance at Biryusa. *Courtesy of VÚA-VHA*

The advance on Kutcherovo was made easier by better quality roads on 3rd June 1919. Austin third series ONDRÁŠ at full-speed. *Courtesy of VÚA-VHA*

JURÁŠ' driver takes advantage of a suitable terrain for speeding. *Courtesy of VÚA-VHA*

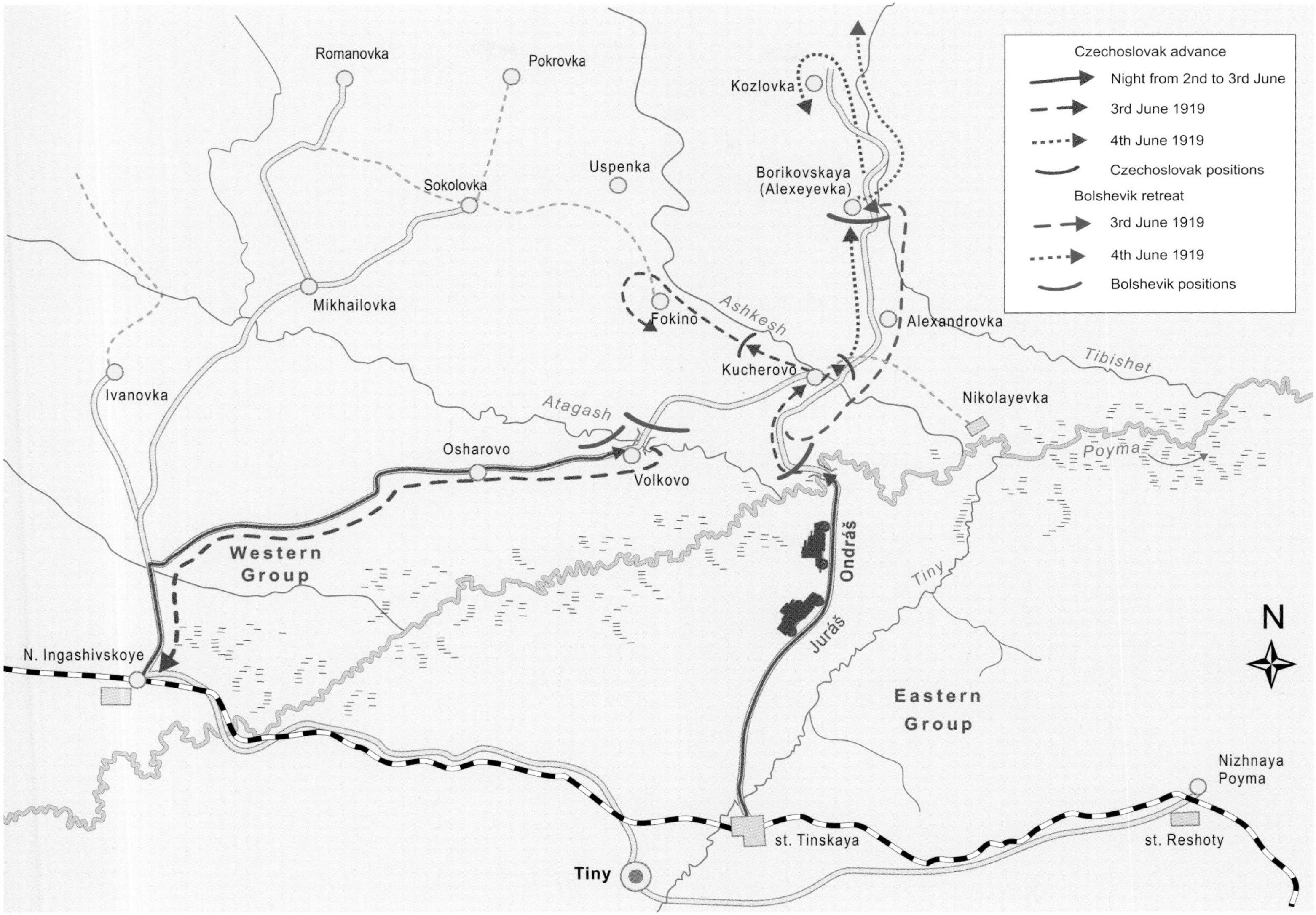

Czechoslovak advance
Night from 2nd to 3rd June
3rd June 1919
4th June 1919
Czechoslovak positions
Bolshevik retreat
3rd June 1919
4th June 1919
Bolshevik positions
Romanovka
Pokrovka
Kozlovka
Uspenka
Sokolovka
Borikovskaya (Alexeyevka)
Mikhailovka
Fokino
Ashkesh
Alexandrovka
Tibishet
Ivanovka
Kucherovo
Atagash
Nikolayevka
Osharovo
Volkovo
Poyma
Western Group
Ondráš
Tiny
Juráš
N
N. Ingashivskoye
Eastern Group
Nizhnaya Poyma
st. Tinskaya
st. Reshoty
Tiny

Operations against the Bolsheviks at the village of Kutcherovo in June 1919. *Hana Rozmanitá, courtesy of ČSOL*

proceeded without resistance through the village of Biryusa to ferry across the river, to provide artillery support to the Western group. After capturing Kontorskoye, the Western group dispersed another guerrilla group and seized documents with plans of enemy bases and further guerrilla tactics. Then the Central group returned to Tayshet through Stary Akulshet.

Between 27th May and 2nd June 1919 Czechoslovak units in Tayshet exchanged Russian armaments for Japanese rifles and machine guns. The attached armored cars, however, retained their original equipment. Guerrillas, expelled from around Tayshet, retreated further from the track to the northwest, and created a new base in the village of Kucherovo, north of the Tinskaya station.

JURÁŠ when passing through a village … *Courtesy of VÚA-VHA*

… and in the captured village of Kutcherovo. JURÁŠ' crew can be seen: Captain Fajfer and volunteer Teplý. *Courtesy of VÚA-VHA*

ONDRÁŠ in Kutcherovo. *Courtesy of VÚA-VHA*

The crews of armored cars and shock troopers before the post office and savings bank in Kutcherovo. Single turreted Austin JURÁŠ no longer has the skull and crossbones motif on its turret. *Courtesy of VÚA-VHA*

JURÁŠ at Irkutsk, carried new markings. It has a white and red ribbon as national insignia, with the name JURÁŠ appearing in white, from the middle of 1919. *Courtesy of VÚA-VHA*

Jeffery-Poplavko JANOŠÍK before the advance on the village of Narva in the Mana River Basin in Siberia, June 1919. The vehicle is marked with a white number 91 on its rear and a red and white ribbon, which is also painted on the backside of the driver's cab. In front of the vehicle its driver, Pfc. Karel Antonín Štěpánek (right) and assistant chauffeur, Pvt. Jan František Šamaj (left). *Courtesy of VÚA-VHA*

Soldiers of the 11th Czechoslovak Rifle Regiment with the armored car JANOŠÍK in the village of Kiyayskoye on the Mana River front in June 1919. *Courtesy of VÚA-VHA*

A red and white ribbon, JANOŠÍK, and the number 91 were also painted on the front. *Courtesy of VÚA-VHA*

Colonel Žák from 2nd to 4th June 1919 commanded an operation against the village of Kucherovo. During the operation a western stream of Czechoslovak units, consisting of battalions from the 2nd and 3rd Czechoslovak Rifle Regiments and the Cavalry Reconnaissance Group of the 3rd Czechoslovak Rifle Regiment, proceeded through the village of Ocharovskoye and Fokino, and encircled Kucherovo from the west and north. The Eastern stream consisted of the 1st, 3rd and 4th companies of the Shock Battalion, three infantry companies, a machine-gun company, an infantry reconnaissance section, two rapid-fire guns of the 2nd Czechoslovak Rifle Regiment, a Machine Gun Company of the 4th Czechoslovak Rifle Regiment, a platoon of horsemen of the mounted battery and both armored cars. It was due to set out on 2nd June 1919 at nine o'clock in the evening from the Tinskaya station to the north and to occupy Kucherovo from the south. Crew of JURÁŠ in this operation consisted of captain Faifer and gunner Teplý.

The western group seized Osharovo, but was stopped in its tracks by a skirmish for a bridge behind the village. The Eastern group was delayed and turned up an hour after midnight on the 3rd June. Felled trees along the route hampered its march. At 11 a.m. the Czechoslovaks at the bridge over the river Poyma clashed with a cover section of about fifty, which was driven out from the trenches by shrapnel. In the afternoon a Czechoslovak cavalry encircled Kucherovo and artillery

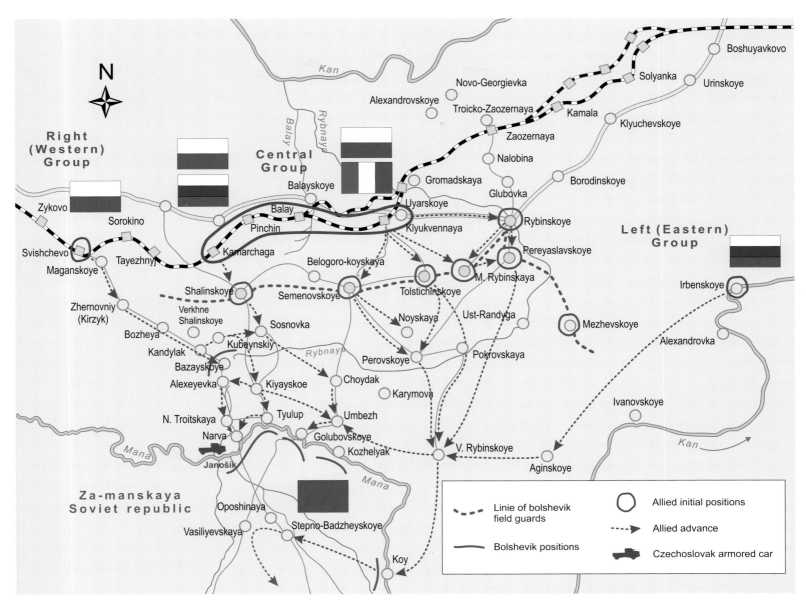

Operations against the Bolsheviks in the Mana River Basin south of Krasnoyarsk, 15th May - 26 June 1919. *Hana Rozmanitá, courtesy of ČSOL*

was fired in several barages against the village. The two armored cars then drove through the village, and took up defensive positions against the Fokinskaya and Borikovskaya villages. However, Bolshevik HQ was warned about this operation by its own reconnaissance and had withdrawn already in the morning from Kucherovo into the village of Borikovskaya. Kucherovo was left deserted. In the village remained only a few people, who did not believe the Bolsheviks warning that the Czechs eat children.

After the Eastern group learned about the failure of the Western group at Osharovo, it spent the night in the village of Kucherovo. On the morning of 4th June it seized Fokino and sent out a cavalry patrol to Alexandrovka and Borikovskaya. The patrol at Borikovskaya clashed with the Bolsheviks, where two were lost and four wounded. The village was deserted but Czechoslovak legionaries found two mutilated corpses of soldiers lost during their morning patrol. After

JANOŠÍK being transported by rail at the Batareynaya station in 1919. *Courtesy of VÚA-VHA*

Armstrong-Whithworth armored car BIVOJ at the 1st Czechoslovak Division's headquarters in autumn of 1919. This is likely to be the Armstrong-Whithworth-Fiat captured at Lipyagi. But it has braided wheels, which was a characteristic of Armstrong-Whithworth armored cars on the Jarrott chassis. The wheels may have been changed in local workshops, but this remains unclear. *Courtesy of VÚA-VHA*

Narva village. *Courtesy of VÚA-VHA*

BIVOJ on flatcars. It carried a red and white ribbon on the front and rear. In white also appears "BIVOJ" on the sides and the rear. *Courtesy of VÚA-VHA*

Austin third series No.209 ONDRÁŠ or SIBIRJAK on a flatcar in 1919. Only red and white ribbons appear on its sides, with no other markings. *Courtesy of VÚA-VHA*

this gruesome discovery they burned the village and returned to Kucherovo. Czechoslovak units returned to Tayshet on 5th June 1919.

Between 15th May and 26th June 1919 a big operation against communist insurgents ran through the area of the 3rd Czechoslovak Rifle Division on the Mana River, southeast of Krasnoyarsk. The following units participated in the operation: the 5th, 9th, 10th and 11th Czechoslovak Rifle Regiments, the 1st Czechoslovak Cavalry Regiment, the 3rd Czechoslovak Artillery Regiment, Italian mountain battalion, Russian Tomsk Hussar Regiment and a Russian rifle battalion. These forces were divided into three groups - frontal, left flank and right (west) flank. They faced around 7,000 men of the Za-manskaya Bolshevik division. On 2nd June the armored car Jeffery-Poplavko JANOŠÍK was detached from the reserve vehicle park and was temporarily attached to the commander of the 3rd Czechoslovak Rifle Division. Its crew consisted of the chauffeur lance corporal Karel Štěpánek and assistant chauffeur private František Šamaj. This armored car mainly supported the 11th Czechoslovak Rifle Regiment, operating from the Kiyayskoye and Narva villages. The operation ended on 26th June 1919 when leaders of the uprising were pushed into Mongolia. Private František Šamaj returned to the reserve Vehicle Park on 10 May 1920, and it is likely that JANOŠÍK remained with the 3rd Division for the remainder of 1919.

The Austin third series at the headquarters of the Car Repair and Maintenance Services of the Czechoslovak Army in Russia in Innokentyevskaya, Irkutsk, 6th December 1919. *Courtesy of VÚA-VHA*

Two Packard freight cars towing an immobile Austin. On the right is a Packard No. 44 with the driver Alois Hradil, followed by the No. 67, with the driver Adalbert Rybnikář. *Courtesy of VÚA-VHA*

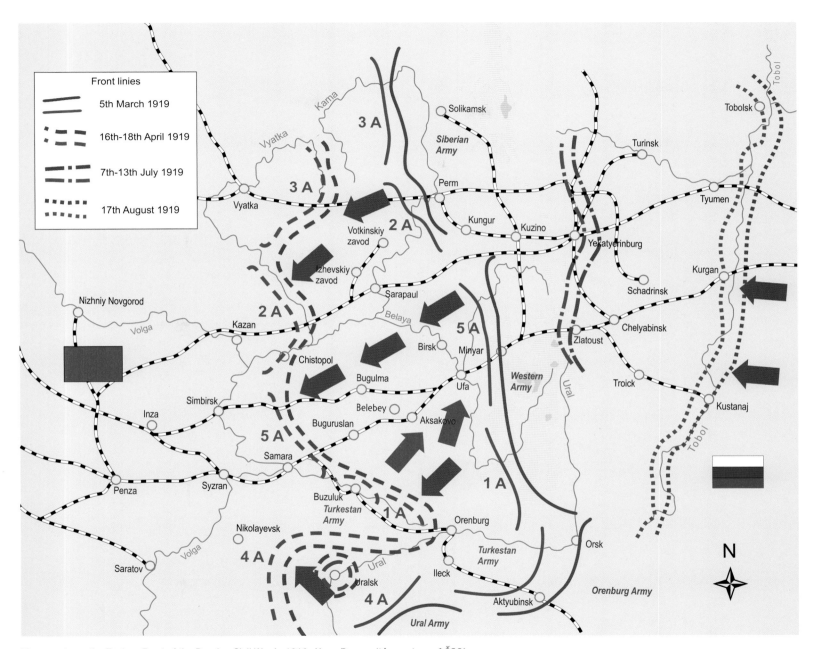

Front linies

—————— 5th March 1919

— ·· — ·· — 16th-18th April 1919

━━ ━━ ━━ 7th-13th July 1919

▪▪▪▪▪ 17th August 1919

3 A

Solikamsk

Siberian Army

Tobolsk

Turinsk

Vyatka

Kama

3 A

Perm

Tyumen

Vyatka

Votkinskiy zavod

2 A

Kungur

Kuzino

Yekaterinburg

Kurgan

Izhevskiy zavod

Sarapaul

Schadrinsk

Nizhniy Novgorod

2 A

Kazan

Belaya

5 A

Chelyabinsk

Volga

Chistopol

Birsk

Minyar

Zlatoust

Troick

Western Army

Ural

Simbirsk

Bugulma

Belebey

Ufa

Kustanaj

Inza

Bug[u]ruslan

Aksakovo

5 A

Samara

1 A

Penza

Syzran

Buzuluk

Turkestan Army

1 A

Orenburg

Nikolayevsk

4 A

Orsk

Saratov

Volga

Ural

Uralsk

Ileck

Turkestan Army

4 A

Aktyubinsk

Orenburg Army

Tobol

Ural Army

N

Movements on the Eastern Front of the Russian Civil War in 1919. *Hana Rozmanitá, courtesy of ČSOL*

Railway transport of the Armored Car Section in the winter of 1919/1920. ONDRÁŠ (left) with horizontal red and white ribbon, JURÁŠ (in the center) with ribbons on its sides and rear and BIVOJ (right). Note variant of the Czechoslovak flag used in Russia in 1919. *Courtesy of VÚA-VHA*

EVACUATION BACK HOME

In April 1919 Kolchak set his offensive on the Volga but was defeated. In June 1919 the Bolsheviks pushed Kolchak's Army back into the Urals. In August 1919 it was pushed back further behind the River Tobol. The "offensive of despair" in September 1919, whose aim was to prevent the Bolsheviks from entering Siberia, brought doom for Kolchak's troops and they were forced to retreat to the east. Starting in the spring of 1919, the Prague government of the Czechoslovak Republic was focused on evacuating the Czechoslovak Army in Russia back to Czechoslovakia, which faced a new threat from Hungarian Bolsheviks. In January 1919, the first transportation carrying disabled soldiers sailed from Vladivostok on the ship Capetown Maru. In December it was followed by the 1st Regiment, after which came other regiments. In February 1920, the Czechoslovak Legion concluded an armistice with the Soviet government and withdrew to Vladivostok. The Czechoslovaks assumed a neutral stance on Japanese intervention in the Far East in spring 1920. Meanwhile Lenin's march towards Europe and for world domination stopped the Russian Volunteer Army of General Wrangel in southern Russia and Ukraine and the Poles and French under polish Field Marshal Pilsudski in front

View of the same railway transportation from the right side. *Courtesy of VÚA-VHA*

Czechoslovak officers with representatives of the Chinese government in front of armored cars in Harbin, May 1920. In the background, from right: Austin third series, Armstrong-Whithworth and single turreted Austin first/second series. *Courtesy of VÚA-VHA*

Embarking in Vladivostok before leaving for home. *Courtesy of VÚA-VHA*

of Warsaw in the summer of 1920. The last Czechoslovak transport left Vladivostok in September 1920. The Russian Far East Republic remained formally independent until 1922, when it was fully absorbed by the Soviet Union. Courtesy of General Gajda, some Czechoslovak weapons were sold to the Korean resistance movement targeted against the Japanese occupation.

There is no evidence to suggest that the Czechoslovak Legion brought back any armored cars from Russia to Czechoslovakia. The Liquidating Department of the Czechoslovak Army in Russia obtained three armored vehicles from the Armored Car Section in Harbin on 10th April 1920. They were: armored car No. 208 Fiat BIVOJ, No. 209 Austin SIBIRJAK and No. 210 Austin JURÁŠ. Already on the 27th April 1920 the Liquidating Department reported that all three cars were sold to the Chinese government for 5,846 Chinese Dollars. The last picture of Czechoslovak armored cars in Russia was taken in Harbin in May 1920. In the background behind the Czechoslovak officers and representatives of the Chinese government stands a line-up of the Austin third series, Armstrong-Whitworth-Fiat and the single-turreted Austin, one of three armored cars whose capturing in Penza, in May 1918, started the history of Czechoslovak "bronyeviks" in Russia.

Motorization at the end of the First World War was still in its infancy. Infantry units consisted of marching units and horse wagons. Pictured for comparison is the Wagon Company of the 1st Czechoslovak Rifle Regiment in Irkutsk. *Courtesy of VÚA-VHA*

AUTOMOTIVE SERVICE OF THE CZECHOSLOVAK ARMY IN RUSSIA

The 1st Czechoslovak aircraft and automobile section was established in February-March 1918 in Kiev as a part of forming the Czechoslovak Rifle Corps. It acquired planes and automobiles from the French military mission, which left Ukraine due to the tumultuous events following the seizure of power by the Bolsheviks. The cars it acquired, however, were few and in poor condition. One month later the automobile platoon of the section, under existing disarmament agreements, left all of its cars and lorries to the Bolsheviks in Krasnoyarsk and Serdobsk. The section was disbanded shortly after arriving in Vladivostok in early June. After the beginning of hostilities with the Bolsheviks, two centers of the Czechoslovak Automotive Service sprung up, in Vladivostok and Yekaterinburg.

The Vladivostok Group of Czechoslovak Rifle Corps was cut-off from other Czechoslovak Groups further west in May-June 1918. It remained neutral up to 29th June 1918, when it disbanded a Bolshevik garrison in Vladivostok and started marching towards the Eastern Group. The same day František Placák summoned former members of the 1st Czechoslovak Aerospace and Automotive Section from various regiments, which also gained one car from the Staff of the 2nd Czechoslovak

Czechoslovak legionaries in Russia made use of all available means, including the most diverse motor vehicles. In this picture can be seen the departure of a motorized pincer section during a skirmish at Tschishima in 1918. *Courtesy of VÚA-VHA*

One key activity performed by the Car Repair and Maintenance Services of the Czechoslovak Army in Russia was to provide fuel and lubricants. In this picture can be seen railroad tanks carrying petrol. *Courtesy of VÚA-VHA*

Rifle Division. One day later he acquired a military garage in Vladivostok, which contained three trucks and two passenger cars. Within a week his unit was in possession of 16 vehicles, of which 14 were in running condition. According to order No. 41 of the Vladivostok Group from 7 July, a new Automotive Section was created under Placák's command in Pyervaya Ryechka in Vladivostok. Its members acquired American cars, originally destined for the Russian Army, which had been stored in crates in a disassembled state for more than two years in Vladivostok. The section also acquired 16 passenger and 60 freight cars. During the reorganization of the 2nd Division, the Section was reorganized into the Independent Automotive Company, on the 3rd September, before moving on to Harbin on 30th August. From there it continued, on 27th October, to Chelyabinsk, where it absorbed an automobile column of the local HQ, and thus strengthened, moved along to Yekaterinburg on 4th December. As of 1 November 1918 the company fell under the command of the Czechoslovak Corps.

A Technical Automotive Section did already exist in Yekaterinburg at the Czechoslovak Corps HQ. According to order No. 102-D from the Military Department of the Czechoslovak National Council's Russian Branch

Car Repair and Maintenance Services of the Czechoslovak Army in Russia's office in Vladivostok. *Courtesy of VÚA-VHA*

Car Repair and Maintenance Services of the Czechoslovak Army in Russia in Vladivostok, spring of 1920. *Courtesy of VÚA-VHA*

(dated 8th September 1918), the Technical Automotive Section was re-organized into the Automotive Section of Czechoslovak Troops. The section was further divided into a combat arm, which was subordinated to Czechoslovak Corps HQ, and a technical section, whose commander was Lieutenant František Alkier (who reported to the Military Department of the Czechoslovak National Council's Russian Branch). The commanders of the combat arm and the technical section enjoyed the rights and obligations of a battalion commander. Warrant Officer Rudolf Thomayer, who was in charge of the chauffeur school and military garages, deputized to second lieutenant Alkier during frequent business trips to Chelyabinsk.

Following the arrival of the Independent Automotive Company in Yekaterinburg, Czechoslovak Corps HQ started reorganizing itself into the Czechoslovak Army in Russia. As a result two units were amalgamated: on 16th December 1918 the Technical Automotive Section was transferred from the purview of the Military Department of the Czechoslovak National Council's Russian Branch to the Corps HQ. On the same day the Reserve Car Park of the Czechoslovak Rifle Corps was established, to which both the Technical Automotive Section and the Independent Automotive Company were subordinated. On 31st December the Technical Automotive Section was disbanded

Trucks had the advantage of a quick bail out, even if a bridge collapsed or in the case of some other kind of accident. In the winter, however, the driver and his assistant were challenged in order to keep sufficiently warm. Selden Truck No. 72, behind the steering wheel sits volunteer Karel Eliška. *Courtesy of VÚA-VHA*

But even drivers of passenger cars in the Russian winter did not suffer by excessive comfort. *Courtesy of VÚA-VHA*

CZECHOSLOVAK ARMORED CARS IN WORLD WAR I AND THE RUSSIAN CIVIL WAR

and amalgamated into the Independent Automotive Company. On 15th January 1919 the Reserve Car Park (Autopark) of the Czechoslovak Army in Russia was established under the command of Placák. Its task was to provide fleets of cars and trucks, spare parts and trained drivers to the Czechoslovak Army in Russia. Warrant Officer 1st Class Placák simultaneously became chief of the Automotive Service Czechoslovak Army in Russia.

In the spring of 1919 all automotive units of the Czechoslovak Army in Russia were gradually reorganized. The Chief of the Automotive Service was responsible for supervising the following an Automobile Park with five automobile columns, the Army Gasoline and Lubricants Store, the Armored Car Section, and automobile sections of all three rifle divisions, the Czechoslovak Army in Russia HQ, the Military Administration of the Far East Area, the Rear Intendance and the authorities of the former Ministry of Military Affairs. One automobile column consisted of sixteen trucks and one passenger car. The Armored Car Section consisted of one motorcycle, one truck and four armored cars. Each automobile section of a rifle division had one motorcycle, two cars and seven trucks. Each of the three rifle divisions also had half an automobile column.

This re-organization was in line with an order covering the Automotive Service of the Czechoslovak Army in Russia prepared by Lieutenant Placák in the summer of 1919, alongside order No. 58 of the Czechoslovak Army in Russia dated 24th August 1919. On that day the Automotive Service had 20 officers, 217 NCOs, 285 ORs and seven civilian employees. The vehicle fleet totaled 64 passenger cars, 103 trucks, 4 armored cars, 5 ambulances, 1 tank truck and 7 motorcycles. According to records, the total number of all vehicles, which passed through its hands, counted 238 cars and 24 motorcycles.

The Autopark was based in Yekaterinburg up to 19th March 1919, when it moved to Irkutsk. From 16th May 1919 to 8th February 1920 it was based at the Innokentyevskaya station near Irkutsk, where it was located in a large railway locomotive shed. With the development of the Russian Civil War it shifted further to the east, first

Officers of the Car Repair and Maintenance Services of the Czechoslovak Army in Russia before evacuation in 1920. Sitting in the middle is František Placák; and seated second from right is Vladimír Kučka. Josef Ruboš stands to the right. *Courtesy of VÚA-VHA*

Staff of the Car Repair and Maintenance Services of the Czechoslovak Army in Russia, 1920. Courtesy of VÚA-VHA

to the Baikal station and then back to Vladivostok, on 26th March 1920. The Autopark Section under the command of 2nd lieutenant Váša and his deputy 2nd lieutenant Ruboš, consisting of two truck columns, was detached from the Autopark in Vladivostok. The task of the Autopark Section was to ensure the evacuation of the remaining Czechoslovak units through the port at Vladivostok. Personnel from the Autopark sailed for home on the USAT Sherman on the 21st May 1920. Part of the Autopark Section was evacuated on the SS President Grant on 19th July 1920, and the rest of it went on the USAT Heffron on 20th September 1920. All of the vehicles from the Autopark were gradually sold off and the proceeds helped to fund the evacuation of Czechoslovak troops. It is unlikely that the legionaries brought back any vehicle from Russia to Czechoslovakia after 1919.

Former members of the Car Repair and Maintenance Services of the Czechoslovak Army in Russia at their reunion in Prague in July 1938. Sitting in the middle is František Placák. *Courtesy of VÚA-VHA*

ING. FRANTIŠEK PLACÁK

František F. Placák was born on 26 August 1886 in the village of Tylovice near Rožnov. He graduated from the Mechanical Engineering Department of the State Higher School, and he learned fluent German, Russian and Polish. He assumed full-time service in the Austro-Hungarian Army on 1st October 1907, and served in the 1st Fortress Artillery Regiment, 3rd Fortress Artillery Battalion, and, finally, in Pola, with the 3rd Fortress Artillery Regiment. At Pola he attained the rank of lieutenant.

He lived in Russia before the war. When he received the mobilization order, he refused to serve in the Austro-Hungarian Army. In 1914-1915 he was the head of various workshops and technical offices at Schöfer-Budenberg in Warsaw, where he oversaw the production of bayonets and fittings for the Russian Navy. At the same time he was head of the Czech Society Beseda in Warsaw at the outbreak of the war. He then participated in the activities of Czech expatriate associations, i.e. care of Czech compatriots, Czech prisoners of war and also, after its establishment, the care of those belonging to the Czech Druzhina. Before the occupation of Warsaw by German troops

on 5th August 1915 he was sent to Perm, where from 1915 to 1916 he worked in the Perm armory and Izhevsk arsenal. In 1916 he was called to St. Petersburg as Chief of Joint Workshops at the Petrograd Technological Institute and Polytechnic Institute. He was given the task to reorganize and increase the plant's production. The factory produced cartridges and fittings. After arriving in St. Petersburg he was involved in the Czech resistance movement. He was a member of the Committee of the Petrograd Czech societies. In this capacity, he was elected in early 1917 as a delegate to the congress of the Union of Czechoslovak Associations in Russia in Kiev. At this Congress he

Captain František Placák in his office in the railway carriage. On his sleeve patch can be seen four silver chevrons denoting the rank of captain and also the Russian automobile units badge made from white metal. Captain Placák is wearing a service belt of western pattern. On the wall in the background is an organizational chart of the Car Repair and Maintenance Services of the Czechoslovak Army in Russia. *Courtesy of VÚA-VHA*

Captain František Placák standing in front of his command wagon. His driver is a Serbian Volunteer, Mirko Dimitrievič, born 11 August 1889 in Kladno, Bohemia (died in 1926 in Bucharest, Romania). *Courtesy of VÚA-VHA*

was elected as a deputy member of the administration of the Union of Czechoslovak Associations in Russia. According to the decision of the congress, chairmen of the main Czechoslovak associations were also members of the Branch of Czechoslovak National Committee in Russia (OČsNR). Because the St. Petersburg chairman Velzl (Welz) was ill (he died soon after the convention), František Placák was appointed his deputy and an OČSNR member. Within the OČSNR he was a member of the organizational and financial commission. He attended the first plenary meeting of the OČSNR held over 14th-18th August 1917 in Moscow, and the second plenary meeting in November-December held in Kiev.

He volunteered for the Czechoslovak Army on 10th August 1917. On 13th December 1917 he was attached to the 1st Artillery Brigade. From 26th February 1918 he was promoted to sergeant and became commander of the Automobile Platoon of the Czechoslovak Corps Headquarters. After leaving for Vladivostok, at the start of operations against the Bolsheviks, he formed the automobile section of the Eastern Group of Czechoslovak troops, which was converted into the Independent Automobile Company on 3rd September. From 1st November 1918 he was responsible for organizing the Automobile Service of the Czechoslovak Rifle Corps. On 1st January 1919 he became commander of the automobile park. On 21st May 1920 he sailed from Vladivostok on the SS Sherman. On 7th July 1920 he crossed the Czechoslovak border. On 29th September 1920 he was assigned to manage the automobile branch of the Czechoslovak Army, where he served in the Automotive Battalion 3. On 1st August 1921 he was assigned to the Automobile Army Reserve. From November 1921 he lived in Liteň near Beroun. His subsequent fate is not known.

Czechoslovak Army: 26th February 1918 Warrant Officer 1st Class, 30th January 1919 Lieutenant, 19th September 1919 Captain, 29th December 1923 allowed to use the title Ing., 28th October 1928 Staff Captain in Reserve, 1st January 1934 First Captain of Artillery in Reserve.

Honors: 24th May 1920 M. R. Štefánik Order Sokol, 1st February 1921 Czechoslovak Military Cross.

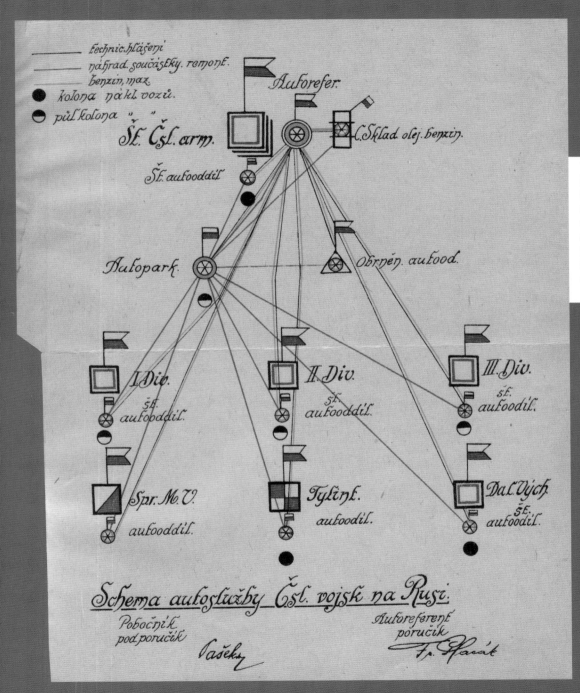

The organizational chart of the Car Repair and Maintenance Services of the Czechoslovak Army in Russia. The black lines show the manner of orders and reporting, the red lines show the workflow of spare parts, and the green lines show the distribution of fuel and lubricants. The full black circle denotes a lorry column, and the half circle stands for a half column. The armored car section is marked as a triangle. *Courtesy of VÚA-VHA*

VLADIMÍR KUČKA

Vladimír Jan Kučka was born on 17th June 1897 in Velké Meziříčí. He attended a grammar school, before applying to study at the engineering department of the Czech Technical University in Brno, but instead of studying he was drafted into the Austro-Hungarian Army at the outbreak of World War I. He served in the Infantry Regiment 3, reached at the rank of Cadet aspirant. He volunteered for the Czechoslovak Legion on 20th February 1918 in POW camp in Zhytomyr, and on the same day he was also assigned to the automobile company of 1st Rifle Division. In photos taken during the first skirmishes of the Penza Group in Penza and Lipyagi he is seen near some captured armored cars. On 13th September 1918 he was assigned to the Technical Automobile Section in Yekaterinburg, where he was assigned an instructor in the Chauffeur School as from 23rd September. After the reorganization of the Czechoslovak Army in Russia, on 1st January 1919 he became a temporary commander of the 3rd column of the Reserve Automobile Park. Between 26th June and 29th September 1919 he studied at a school for officers in Sludyanka. On 20th January 1920 he was appointed commander of the Armored Car Section.

At the beginning of 1920 he was one of the founders of the Enyergiya co-operative with an engineering and business program together with A. Váša, Vl. Ottmar, J. Ruboš and K. Marek. This co-operative was engaged in the rental and sale of Czechoslovak military equipment, which could not be transported to Czechoslovakia. He was evacuated to Czechoslovakia on the ship "Keenan." He was one of six men whom František Placák

Second Lieutenant Vladimír Jan Kučka. *Courtesy of VHÚ*

thanked for fulfilling duties in the service of the Czechoslovak Army in Russia in order No. 134 of 5th March 1921, the last order issued by the Automobile Park.

In Czechoslovakia he was assigned to the 1st Automobile Battalion. From 1923 to 1929 Vladimír Kučka successfully represented the Czechoslovak Republic and its Army in motorcycle races at home and abroad. Together with František Chlad, Čeněk and Alžběta Junek and V. Liška, he came first in several international competitions. He achieved some of his biggest successes on the machines Walter AJS 350 and 500, Indian 1000, and, chiefly, the Brough Superior SS 100, which was purchased for him in the UK by the Czechoslovak Ministry of National Defence. On 9th October 1924 he became one of the founding members of the Union of Competitors, and in 1927 he was its first Vice-President. After 1929 he became a civilian. Along with his friend Vladimir Ottmar he founded the Autorama car-repair company which became successful in its branch. Vladimír Kučka died in 1941 in an unexplained car accident. He died as a result of internal injuries two days later after a backing truck pinned him to a wall in his workshop in Holešovice.

He died relatively young, at the age of 44. According to witnesses, he was an elegant and sociable man. He spoke Russian, German and French. He was also an avid photographer who took many of the unique images of the Czechoslovak Legion fighting in Russia and Siberia during the war.

Estates title Ing., 14th September 1918 Corporal, 6th December 1918 on the occasion of announcement of Czechoslovakia independence promoted to Technical Sergeant-Major, 4th April 1919 Deputy Officer, 8th May 1919 Master Sergeant, 28th September 1919 2nd Lieutenant, 1920 Captain, 1928 Staff Captain.

Honors: 3rd August 1919 British War Medal, 20th May 1920 Russian Cross of St. George 4th class.

Vladimír Kučka in Harbin with a Japanese geisha, Oiosa Khutikosu. On his sleeve patch can be seen a red triangle, the same as for a shock battalion, but instead of a skull and crossbones, as worn by shock troopers, he dons a badge denoting Russian automobile units with white metal. *Courtesy of VÚA-VHA*

Captain Vladimír Kučka as a motorcycle racer in 1929. *Author's collection*

INDEPENDENT ARMORED CAR SECTION PERSONNEL IN 1920

Surname	Name	Ranked	Inactivated	Note
Austen	Bedřich		22nd April 1920	
Barcal	František			Driver's assistant of armored car No. 209 ONDRÁŠ or SIBIRJAK at 2nd Rifle Division.
Čapek	Antonín		26th February 1920	Driver of armored car Armstrong-Whitworth-Fiat No. 208 BIVOJ at 1st Rifle Division and Czechoslovak Army in Russia HQ Evacuated for homeland on 26th February 1920.
Dlouhý	Čeněk	20th January 1920	22nd April 1920	
Hudec	Josef	20th January 1920	4th February 1920	
Hradil	Alois	20th January 1920	22nd April 1920	
Kepka	František			Driver of Austin armored car No. 209 ONDRÁŠ or SIBIRJAK at 2nd Rifle Division.
Kučka	Vladimír	20th January 1920	22nd April 1920	Section Commander
Kneisel	František		22nd April 1920	also mentioned as Kneisl
Poborský	Václav	27th January 1920	22nd April 1920	
Procházka	František	20th January 1920	22nd April 1920	
Pícha	Josef	20th January 1920	22nd April 1920	also mentioned as Pýcha
Pinsker	Innocenc		22nd April 1920	also mentioned as Pilsker
Sandner	Alfons	20th January 1920	22nd April 1920	
Štěpánek	Karel			Driver of Jeffery-Poplavko armored car No. 91 JANOŠÍK at 3rd Rifle Division.
Šubert	František		22nd April 1920	also mentioned as Schubert
Švanda	Josef		26th February 1920	Driver of Austin armored car No. 210 JURÁŠ at Czechslovak Arrmy in Russia HQ. Evacuated for homeland on 26th February 1920
Vilikovský	Josef	20th January 1920	22nd April 1920	also mentioned as Velikovský
Vurmser	Ludvík			also mentioned as Wurmser
Zbořil	Karel	20th January 1920	22nd April 1920	
Zikmund	František		22nd April 1920	

Garford heavy armored car, captured by soldiers of the 1st Czechoslovak Rifle Regiment in Penza, Russia on 28th May 1918, and then used by the 4th Czechoslovak Rifle Regiment. It was camouflaged in green. On both sides, front and rear, the name GROZNIY (in Russian "Terrible") appeared in shades of yellow and black, which dated from the time when the machine was used by the 15th machine gun truck platoon of the Russian Imperial Army. *Petr Štěpánek, courtesy of ČSOL*

CAMOUFLAGE AND MARKING

There is a consensus among researchers about camouflage paint used on Russian armored vehicles during World War I that nobody seems to know anything about it. Contemporary sources describe their color in terms like "dark green," "yellow ocher" or "grass green." In terms of Czechoslovak vehicles, little is known about the color of the Garford, Fiat-Izhorskis and on the single-turreted Austin. Armored cars imported to Russia from the United Kingdom were painted British green, but little is known about the colors of British vehicles in World War I as well.

The marking of Czechoslovak bronyeviks was initially either their original one or (most often) none. The Garford GROZNIY had his name painted in probably yellow letters with black shading. In order to prepare for the disintegration of the Russian Army, a movement of so-called death units emerged in the summer of 1917. Their insignia was a skull and crossbones, which expressed willingness of these soldiers to fight for their homeland, to the death if necessary. The armored Austin vehicle was marked in this way, which had on the left-hand side of its turret a white skull and crossbones. The Bolsheviks left this

The armored car Jeffery-Poplavko, used by troops of the 3rd Czechoslovak Rifle Division at the village of Narva in the Mana River Basin in Siberia in May and June 1919, had the white name JANOŠÍK on its sides. The front and rear bore the white number 91 and a red and white ribbon, which also appeared on the backside of the driver's cab. *Petr Štěpánek, courtesy of ČSOL*

The Czechoslovak Austin third series was also camouflaged with a single color, probably green. Horizontal red and white ribbons also appeared with a broad white stripe. *Petr Štěpánek, courtesy of ČSOL*

marking unchanged. It was in this form that the single-turreted Austin was captured in Penza by the Czechoslovak Legions, and which participated in the struggle for Penza. It was present during ORLÍK's collision with the "wild" engine behind the Alexandrovsky Bridge on 31st May 1918. The skull-and-crossbones marking is mentioned again before the evacuation of Samara on 2nd October 1919. The last picture was taken in the summer of 1919 in Siberia. It was later painted over.

Even in 1918 Czechoslovak armored cars had a little red and white flag on their bonnet. Standardized markings on Czechoslovak armored vehicles begin to emerge in the autumn of 1919. This was probably the result of the following order, Czechoslovak Corps No. 47, from 16th April 1918, targeted at uniforms–accordingly, the Russian cockade was removed from peak and winter caps, and replaced with ribbons in national colors, red and white. The ribbon was 1-2 cm in width, sewn diagonally at an angle of 60 degrees, the upper left and lower right (from wearer's point of view). The length of the ribbons was based on the width of the cap's sides; for winter caps its length was 4 cm. Rhombus ribbons of similar proportions, but larger, bore the "JANOŠÍK" armored car. On the Austin third series and on the Armstrong-Whitworth-Fiat ribbons were painted, with white on the upper two thirds and red on the lower third.

Freight and passenger cars of the Czechoslovak Legion in Russia were marked with a one- to three-digit, black, or white number, on their fronts, and on the grille. The numbers of armored vehicles starting in 1919 were 91, 208, 209 and 210, but only JANOŠÍK bore the painted white number 91 on its front and rear.

The Bolshevik Austin, destroyed at Khrompik by Czechoslovak stormtroopers, also bore interesting markings. On the sides it had two red-blue-white circular cockades. This was the national marking for armored vehicles from the time of the Russian Republic in 1917, which remained unchanged by new users. According to some photographs, it is likely that the single-turreted Austin carried it on its rear under the turret with the same emblem painted over.

TABLE OF KNOWN ARMORED VEHICLES, USED BY CZECHOSLOVAK LEGIONARIES IN RUSSIA

	Date	Place	Type	Original marking	Czechoslovak Name	Czecho-slovak Evidence No.	Written off	Place	Note
1	28th May 1918	Penza	Single-Turreted Austin first/second series	Skull and Bones	JURÁŠ	210.	10th April 1920	Kharbin	Sold to China.
2	28th May 1918	Penza	Armstrong-Whitworth-Fiat				31st May 1918	Obsharovka	Destroyed after crash of improvised armored train ORLÍK with "wild" unmanned steam engine.
3	28th May 1918	Penza	Garford	ГРОЗНЫЙ (GROZNIY)			3rd October 1918	Batraki	Abandoned in front of Alexandrovsky Bridge during retreat.
4	2nd June 1918	Bezenchuk	? with two machine-guns"				?	?	= Austin third series ONDRÁŠ ?
5	4th June 1918	Lipyagi	Armstrong-Whitworth-Fiat		BIVOJ	208.	10th April 1920	Kharbin	Sold to China.
6	4th June 1918	Lipyagi	Fiat-Izhorski	36.			?	?	
7	5th June 1918	Bezenchuk	?				?	?	= Austin third series ONDRÁŠ ?
8	6th June 1918	Marianovka	Benz				?	?	
9	9th June 1918	Tatarskaya	?				?	?	
10	17th June 1918	Troitsk	?				17th June 1918	Troitsk	Destroyed enemy vehicle. Captured wreck.
11	17th June 1918	Troitsk	?				17th June 1918	Troitsk	Destroyed enemy vehicle. Captured wreck.
12	17th June 1918	Troitsk	Fiat-Izhorski				?	?	
13	26th June 1918	Buzuluk	?				26th June 1918	Buzuluk	Destroyed enemy vehicle. Captured wreck.

	Date	Place	Type	Original marking	Czechoslovak Name	Czecho-slovak Evidence No.	Written off	Place	Note
14	26th June 1918	Buzuluk	?				26th June 1918	Buzuluk	Destroyed enemy vehicle. Captured wreck.
15	26th June 1918	Buzuluk	Fiat-Izhorski				?	?	Wreck without engine.
16	29th June 1918	Zlokazovo	Garford	ВИТЯЗЬ (VITYAZ)			29th June 1918	Zlokazovo	Destroyed enemy vehicle. Captured wreck.
17	4th July 1918	Vagay	Fiat-Izhorski				4th July 1918	Vagay	Destroyed enemy vehicle. Captured wreck.
18	19th July 1918	Briandino	?	VENOMOUS			?	?	
19	20th July 1918	Briandino	?				?	?	
20	22nd July 1918	Khrompik	Austin 2nd series	Former Russian cockade			22nd July 1918	Khrompik	Destroyed enemy vehicle. Captured wreck.
21	6th August 1918	Kazan	?				6th August 1918	Kazan	Destroyed enemy vehicle. Captured wreck.
22	6th August 1918	Kazan	?				?	?	
23	6th August 1918	Sarga	Jeffery-Poplavko		JANOŠÍK	91.	?	?	
24	17th August 1918	Posolskaya	Fiat-Izhorski (?)				?	?	Captured with damaged engine and machine-guns.
25	?	?	Austin third series		ONDRÁŠ, SIBIRJAK	209.	10th April 1920	Kharbin	Sold to China.

Volunteer of Czech Druzhina Antonín Grmela in the picture taken in August or September 1914. Grmela is wearing a white-red ribbon around the flange of service cap of Russian origin. He is wearing rubashka Mark 1912. Epaulettes are of camouflage (grey-green) color with laces of Russian one-year volunteer. Some Czechoslovak volunteers mistakenly deemed it as a sign for all volunteers in the Russian Army and sewed-in such insignia on their epaulettes just to be ordered to rip it off. Grmela is wearing shipcloth trousers and high leather boots. There is nothing except of white-red ribbon to differentiate Grmela from Russian soldiers of that period. Antonín Grmela was captured in Galicia on 9th December 1914 on his journey to homeland with the task to pass messages to home resistance. He was executed in Vadovice on 12th December 1914. *Courtesy of VÚA-VHA*

Volunteer of Czech Druzhina Jezbera, August or September 1914. Epaulettes on his overcoat for enlisted men of infantry are of raspberry color. One row of yellow metal buttons still remains in front of it. Those buttons were painted over with camouflage color or removed later in the war. Even epaulettes were often removed from overcoats. *Courtesy of VÚA-VHA*

UNIFORMS OF ARMORED CAR CREWS BELONGING TO CZECHOSLOVAK LEGIONS IN RUSSIA

Members of the Czechoslovak rifle brigade, enlisted men and officers, doctors and military clerks met the beginning of 1917 year wearing uniforms and equipment of Russian Army, which fully reflected its regulations and naturally corresponded to its partially limited war supply capabilities. The description of parts of Russian uniforms and equipment, which were used by Czechoslovak units, is far beyond the content of this book. To fully understand this topic we recommend studying specialized sources written in Russian. Cockades worn on the various headgear and shoulder straps were an integral part of Russian uniforms. Those cockades were different for enlisted men, officers, medical staff and for military clerks. By the shoulder strap it was possible to recognize the rank and unit, respectively branch of forces, sometimes whether the bearer of such epaulettes belonged to a specialized unit within a higher formation (e.g. machinegun units members within infantry regiments).

When speaking about members of armored car formations within the Russian Army, their insignia is directly linked to insignia of automobile units of this army. The first use of cars was recorded during Russian Army exercises in 1897, when Admiralty tested a bunch of cars. More than 15 various cars took part in exercises in 1902 and a bunch of cars was acquired by the Ministry of Military Affairs for Main Headquarters and for Feldyegerski Corps. Cars were used during the Russian–Japanese war. The Imperial School of Drivers was established in 1906 and some automobile fortification units were formed later. A plan to form a couple of automobile companies belonging to the railway battalions was accepted in 1908 and the 1st Training Automobile Company was established in 1910. The development continued and the war accelerated it.

Rifleman of 1st Czechoslovak Regiment. Czechoslovak soldiers started to use regular Russian lettering "ЧС" on their epaulettes shortly after Czechoslovak Rifle Regiment formation and later they combined those letters even with the appropriate regiment number. Such numbers were usually used till the end of 1917 when removal of epaulettes was ordered. There is a piece of white-red ribbon fixed next to the cockade on the cap. *Author's collection*

Second Lieutenant Zach, belonging to 1st Czechoslovak Regiment. He is wearing a field service cap with officer's cockade without any piece of white-red ribbon. Such omission of national insignia from time to time appeared amongst both officers and enlisted men. Second Lieutenant Zach is wearing a French jacket. His officer's epaulettes are marked with "1ЧС" lettering. *Courtesy of VÚA-VHA*

Sgt. Beneš, Polonoe, 1917, regimental tailor of 3rd Regiment, in his best dress. There is an improvised Czechoslovak cockade with a lion on his field cap. Such cockade appeared during the second half of 1917. He is wearing the French jacket of pristine officer's shape. Black epaulettes are laced with probably white-red but not surely identified trim. Rank of Sergeant Beneš is denoted by the three rank stripes on "colorful" or "peacetime" epaulette of white color prescribed by regulations. Complete appearance is topped by epaulette button of proper dimensions as given by regulations, red shipcloth chalice and Russian number "3." *Courtesy of VÚA-VHA*

First members of automobile units were transferred mainly from railway troops staff and wore their uniforms. But the necessity to introduce specialized dress, equipment and insignia soon became apparent. Such equipment and insignia were introduced for the 1st Training Automobile Company by the Instruction of the Ministry of Military Affairs No. 131 issued on 19th March 1911 (of the Julian Calendar, which was at that time used in Russia). It is not necessary to describe full content of that instruction so only specific details of automobile service will be mentioned here.

This instruction introduced a peaked cap with flat visor, which did not obstruct the driver's view. Every driver was proud of his goggles. Additional parts of uniform, e.g. so called Swedish jackets, made of brown leather and brown leather trousers, were introduced. The same instruction mentioned later insignia of automobile troops – two wheels with a steering wheel and wings, which is used even nowadays not only in Russia. The majority of equipment as well as the insignia were introduced to the rest of the automobile companies and units by the Instruction of the Ministry of Military Affairs No. 367 issued on 12th July 1913 (of the Julian Calendar). It was difficult to issue new uniforms to all the

Cropped photo. Lance Corporal of 5th Czechoslovak Regiment, member of Staff of Training Detachment of 5th Czechoslovak Regiment. Borispol, December 1917. He is wearing a winter cap with cockade without white-red ribbon. He is dressed in overcoat with two rows of buttons, which were made for enlisted men from autumn 1917. Russian number "5" is recognizable on his epaulettes. Some of legionaries again used trim of various colors in 1917. Former Austro-Hungarian officers were sent to various classes to confirm their ability and graduate to become officers again. Those officers were frequently but mistakenly called one-year volunteers and were using their Russian insignia. Plain legionaries belonging to various Czechoslovak regiments started to wear red and white woven trim. *Author's collection*

A rifleman of 3rd Czechoslovak Regiment accompanied by a driver belonging to unknown unit, Orvanitse, 1917. The driver is wearing shipcloth cap with flat visor, so called Swedish jacket and leather trousers. Insignia of Russian automobile units is visible on his epaulettes. There are some numbers and lettering visible on one of his epaulettes. Those are stencilled with oil paint. The number could be "82" with certain probability. The driver could be either Russian or Czech driver attached to the Staff of Czechoslovak brigade or even a Czech driver serving with Russian automobile unit. *Courtesy of VÚA-VHA*

Drivers Vaněk, V. Medek, Jirutka and Schejbal attached to HQ of Czechoslovak Brigade, Bereznice, distillery, 1917. The drivers in the picture are wearing three different types of rubashka blouses. Medek is wearing something like a variation of French jacket. Schejbal standing far right is wearing a regular Russian field cap. The rest are wearing a mix of Russian field cap imitations ,and Medek is probably wearing an imitation of Russian driver's cap. There are insignia of Russian automobile units made of metal visible on epaulettes of Vaněk and Jirutka. *Courtesy of VÚA-VHA*

members of Russian automobile units due to the lack of material during the war. Factories and shops without having any previous experience of such production produced certain parts of uniforms and equipment, e.g. so called Swedish jackets. This resulted in some deviations from regulations. Leather of lower quality was frequently used for production.

The first armored car appeared in Russia in 1906, but after a couple of years of tests it was not accepted for service in the armed forces. There was no armored cars unit within the Russian Army till the outbreak of war, but the situation has changed. Staff of 5th and 8th automobile companies built improvised armored cars before those were sent to the frontline in the autumn 1914. The project developed by 1st automobile machinegun company was presented at the end of August 1914. Soldiers of this

Rifleman Blahut, a dispatch rider of HQ of Czechoslovak Rifle Brigade, Polonoe, September 1917. Blahut is wearing a shipcloth cap and goggles for drivers. He is dressed in rubashka blouse. There is an insignia of Russian automobile units made of metal visible on his epaulettes. His belt is interesting too – it is an Austro-Hungarian belt including the buckle. *Courtesy of VÚA-VHA*

unit went to the battle on 9th November 1914 (of the Julian Calendar). The development of more armored cars units started in a short time.

First members of armored car formations were equipped with a full set of leather clothes for battle service, which did not vary according to photographs from so called Swedish jackets and above mentioned leather trousers issued to automobile units. They were equipped with caps of special shape with flat visor and earflaps. Some Russian sources mention those caps as

Mark 1911 caps, previously introduced for motorized elements of engineer forces. Insignia of machinegun units superimposed to insignia of automobile service appeared in the shoulder straps of armored car unit's members. Then there was a company number worn below those two insignia in the shoulder strap. Then there was new special insignia introduced by the Instruction of the Ministry of Military Affairs No. 328 issued in 1915. This special insignia amalgamated both the automobile and machinegun insignias

mentioned above. But of course not all new members of such units were due to war shortages equipped with all parts of uniforms and equipment as required by regulations.

Since 1914 white–red ribbon worn on the cap was an insignia of Czechoslovak volunteers belonging to the Russian Imperial Armed Forces. Those are colors of the Czech Kingdom heraldic emblem – a silver lion on the red shield. A piece of white-red ribbon was pinned and worn below the Russian cockade on different service caps in 1917, but not only below it, it was pinned also next to or even across that cockade. At the end of 1917 Czechoslovak soldiers were issued with at least several hundreds of Czechoslovak cockades with a lion made of metal. Such insignia with ribbon and cockade was officially used till April 1918.

Lettering „ČS," written in the Cyrillic Alphabet as „ЧС," appeared on the epaulettes of Czechoslovak units when Czecho-Slovak Rifle Regiment was formed in 1916 and later, when more regiments were raised, the lettering was changed to „1ЧС," „8ЧС" etc. In 1917, some units started to use the symbol of the medieval religious Hussite movement – the chalice – in their shoulder straps. The form and any other requirements of epaulettes used by Czechoslovak soldiers, officers and military clerks corresponded to Russian regulations. Unfortunately there is not enough space for a more detailed description.

Rank insignia in use form January to October 1918
Introduced by Czechoslovak Rifle Corps Order No 15
(an example of 1st Czechoslovak Rifle Regiment)

Rifleman

Lance Corporal

Note:

1st Row - Men
2nd Row - NCOs
3rd Row - Company NCOs
4th Row - Staff Officers
5. řada 5th Row - Generals

Corporal

Sergeant

Sergeant Major

Warrant Officer 2nd Class

W. O. 1st Class

2nd Lieutenant

Lieutenant

Staff Captain

Captain

Lt. Colonel

Colonel

Major General

Lt. General

General

Courtesy of Jiři Charfreitag

Group of 5th Rifle Regiment soldiers, before the end of October 1918. Soldiers are wearing Russian field caps, without cockades now. White-red ribbons from April 1918 replaced those. Soldiers sitting in the center and standing on the far right have left shoulder shield patches, without laces following orders in force at that period. Soldier on the right has got non-regular shape of shield and besides number "5", he is wearing Russian insignia of phone and telegraph operators – crossed lightnings – and belongs to telephone detachment of regiment. *Author's collection*

Lieutenant Bedřich Homola, Officer of 6th Czechoslovak Regiment. He is wearing non-regular rubashka blouse with left shoulder shield patch laced with raspberry color, rank insignia and Russian regular number "6." *Courtesy of VHÚ-VHA*

Assault soldier, member of Shock Battalion. Perfect example of a soldier who does not obey regulations – under the triangle the not laced left shoulder shield patch made of cloth (the same material from which rubashka blouse is made) with rank insignia is missing. By wearing white-red ribbon on his chest this assault soldier denotes clearly that he belongs to Czechoslovak Army. *Courtesy of VÚA-VHA*

Second Lieutenant Antonín Halbich from 3rd Company of Shock Battalion. He is wearing French jacket and first variant of Shock Battalion insignia is visible on his left sleeve. Left shoulder shield patch is made of the same material as the French jacket was made (camouflage, probably grey-green) laced in raspberry color. Halbich was killed in action near Utkinsky factory in Urals on 6th September 1918. *Courtesy of VÚA-VHA*

Members of Shock Battalion wearing Adrian helmets. Some of them decorated their helmets with skull and crossed bones others used white-red ribbons. Courtesy of VÚA-VHA

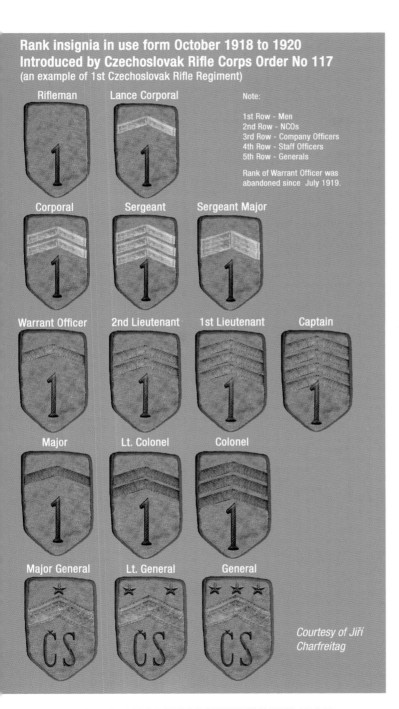

Rank insignia in use form October 1918 to 1920
Introduced by Czechoslovak Rifle Corps Order No 117
(an example of 1st Czechoslovak Rifle Regiment)

Rifleman	Lance Corporal

Note:

1st Row - Men
2nd Row - NCOs
3rd Row - Company Officers
4th Row - Staff Officers
5th Row - Generals

Rank of Warrant Officer was
abandoned since July 1919.

Corporal	Sergeant	Sergeant Major

Warrant Officer	2nd Lieutenant	1st Lieutenant	Captain

Major	Lt. Colonel	Colonel

Major General	Lt. General	General

Courtesy of Jiří Charfreitag

Group of soldiers and an officer belonging to 1st Czechoslovak Regiment, period after October 1918. Staff Sergeant on the right seems to be the most interesting. He is dressed in French jacket. His left shoulder shield patch is laced as was introduced in October 1918. There are Russian (used from December 1916) and Czechoslovak (used from October 1918) ribbons for two wounds. Time of service insignia in the form introduced in October 1918 is visible on his right sleeve. *Courtesy of VÚA-VHA*

Captain belonging to 1st Czechoslovak Regiment. He is wearing French jacket with a left shoulder shield patch laced in raspberry color, rank of Captain insignia and number "1" of later pattern or of non-Russian origin. Ribbons for wounds are visible on the left lower sleeve. He was once wounded during his enlisted men service years and twice as an officer. *Courtesy of VÚA-VHA*

Any instruction or an order dealing with insignia of newly formed Czechoslovak automobile units within Czechoslovak Corps has not been discovered yet. We can answer such a question only with knowledge of a couple of documents and orders issued for similar Russian formations and a few taken photographs. Since 1915 minimum quantities of automobile equipment were listed for units and formations of different size within Russian Armed Forces. Every Army should have two Automobile Companies and a Motorcycle Platoon in their table of organization. There were listed six passenger cars, one lorry and two motorcycles attached to Corps Headquarters, two passenger cars and four motorcycles attached to Infantry Division headquarters and two motorcycles attached to Regiment headquarters. Similarly armored cars belonging to different automobile machinegun companies were detached to formations at various levels.

An automobile detachment with six lorries was planned amongst various elements to be attached to the Heavy Artillery Battalion of Czechoslovak Corps according to project by Capt. Jaroslav Červinka in 1917. There were Czechoslovak Automobile Ambulance Company with ten vehicles, Czechoslovak Aviation Battalion with two passenger cars and certainly with planes, and in particular there was Czechoslovak Armored Car Battalion listing three Austin or Fiat armored cars armed with machineguns, one Garford armored car armed with gun

and with three machineguns, 4 lorries and four motorcycles including one of them with sidecar and two bikes.

Enlisted men and officers of the Automobile Detachment attached to Park of Heavy Artillery Battalion and personnel of the Automobile Ambulance Company should wear appropriate Russian insignia on their epaulettes but we can successfully question the use of appropriate insignia of "army automobile ambulance troops" in the form as was in theory introduced by the Instruction of the Ministry of Military Affairs No.565 issued on 29. August 1917 (of the Julian Calendar).

If we were to speculate, then there should be above mentioned special Russian insignia of armored car units on the epaulettes of field (camouflaged) color with buttons appropriate for engineer units (with eagle and two crossed axes), made of white metal and painted over with camouflage color or with button either made of wood or of leather with four holes and painted over with bright green oil paint worn by enlisted men and non-commissioned officers of the Armored Car Section, as planned for Czechoslovak Corps. Then below those insignia there should be lettering „ЧС" in bright green oil paint. We have to mention some Russian sources stating that in 1916 there was a change from bright green to red for armored car formations.

There should be above mentioned special Russian insignia of armored car units made of white metal or embroidered in the officers silverish epaulettes with red stitching (red epaulette with silver

galloon) with buttons appropriate for engineer units (with eagle and two crossed axes), made of white metal and lettering „ЧС" made of yellow metal worn by officers of the same unit. We can say with the highest probability that officers would prefer wearing a field variant of shoulder straps with buttons overpainted with camouflage color and with special insignia, numbers and rank pips/stars subdued.

There is pictorial evidence of Czechoslovak soldiers wearing only special insignia of automobile units on their epaulettes in 1917, especially by motorcycle riders attached to headquarters of Czechoslovak units of various levels. A photograph of Czechoslovak officer wearing special automobile units insignia made of metal on his epaulettes has not been discovered yet. It is hard to believe that one day a picture of a Czechoslovak soldier of any rank wearing insignia of armored car units would be discovered.

We have learned from all available sources that the processing of automobile units' formation within Czechoslovak Corps started at the beginning of 1918. It is necessary to take into account that there was established Joint Czechoslovak Aviation and Automobile Detachment at the very beginning. It is difficult to deduce whether such a formation could have its own uniform insignia. Such insignia should not be worn on the epaulettes.

A difficult situation followed the Bolshevik coup at the end of 1917, and led to the withdrawal of Russia from the war. By the decision of new Russian leaders, declared on 10th November

1917 (of the Julian Calendar) all ranks, titles, shoulder straps and medals were cancelled without any replacement with effect from 3rd December 1917. All previous talks about projects of Czechoslovak epaulettes were interrupted. It was ordered to remove epaulettes by the Order No. 15 issued by the Czechoslovak Corps Headquarters dated 30th December 1917 (12thJanuary of the Gregorian Calendar) and the same order introduced shield patches to be worn on the left upper arm sleeve. The quantity and color of stripes in the shape of reversed letter V (chevrons) positioned on that left sleeve shield patch were to denote the rank. Military clerks wore horizontal stripes instead of chevrons. Special insignia and number worn on the patch denoted which unit a soldier belonged to. Cyrillic Alphabet letters were used to denote units of Czechoslovak Corps. Numbers, special insignia for enlisted men, non-commissioned officers and warrant officers up to Chief Warrant Officer CW-1 were ordered to be painted in the left sleeve shield patch in accordance with Russian rules with yellow oil paint; those numbers were made of metal or embroidered for officers, doctors and military clerks. It is hardly to find

Lieutenant belonging to Shock Battalion wearing French jacket with left shoulder shield patch laced in raspberry color. The left shoulder shield patch is in its final form as was introduced in October 1918. Red left shoulder shield patch is laced in raspberry color, there is rank insignia and the skull and crossed bones. *Courtesy of VÚA-VHA*

Group of students of school for officers attached to 1st Czechoslovak Cavalry Regiment "Jana Jiskry z Brandýsa", Yekaterinburg, photo dated 28th February 1919. There is school commander, former Sotnik of Siberian Cossack Army and First Sergeant of Czechoslovak Armed Forces (promoted at the end of December 1918) Nikolaj Matvějev sitting in the center and wearing a darker form of kitel jacket. This school was established on 7th January 1919 and last exams were done on 20th and 23rd March 1919. All soldiers wear a winter variant of Czechoslovak Cavalry cap called Podyebradka (with regular white brush), which was introduced to 1st Cavalry Regiment in February 1919. Within 1st Cavalry Regiment this cap was used as ceremonial headgear only (unlike 2nd Cavalry Regiment). Some of the students wear their kitel jackets made in the style of Russian cavalry short jackets including sleeves being cuffed by reversed V cuffs. *Courtesy of VÚA-VHA*

painted insignia numbers in available pictures as a majority of Czechoslovak soldiers wore numbers made of metal, special insignia and letters. Left sleeve shield patches for enlisted men, non-commissioned officers and warrant officers up to Chief Warrant Officer CW-1 were not laced. Left sleeve shield patches worn by all officers and members of OČsNR were laced by galloon of raspberry color, left sleeve shield patches worn by vice-officers (one-year volunteers) were laced by black-white-yellow galloon, and doctors and military clerks had their left sleeve shield patches laced by red galloon. Military doctors, veterinarians and military clerks were gradually promoted to the ranks of officers of this or that branch or service. Russian uniforms remained in use.

Separation of Czechoslovak Corps from the slowly perishing Russian Armed Forces had political dimension, too. The Branch of Czechoslovak National Committee in Russia (OČsNR) in accordance to agreement with French authorities declared on 25th January 1918 (7th February 1918 of the Gregorian Calendar – 31st January 1918 was last day of the Julian Calendar, then the Gregorian Calendar followed with 14th February 1918) *"Czechoslovak Forces in all regions of former Russian state to be part of autonomous Army in France."* Since that day all the care for equipment and armament of Czechoslovak legionaries were fully in Czech hands.

National insignia of Czechoslovak legionaries was adjusted by the Order of Czechoslovak Corps, No. 47 issued on 16th April 1918, by *which "all brothers were ordered to remove cockades from their caps and winter headgear and replace those with ribbon of Czech national colors 1-2 centimeters wide. Length of ribbon should be enough according to the cap flange height to allow the ribbon to be sewn-in diagonally at 60 degrees from top left to bottom right; length of ribbon to be worn on fur cap should be 4 centimeters."*

Order No. 15, which introduced left sleeve shield patches, was gradually complemented in connection to the start of fighting Bolsheviks, which led to the formation of important numbers of newly formed units of Czechoslovak Corps. The most complex adjustment of Order No. 15 was implemented by the Order of Czechoslovak Corps No. 117 dated 27th October 1918. The rank of Staff Captain war renamed Captain and the rank of Captain was changed to Major. Position of vice-officer (one-year volunteer) and the rank of Chief Warrant Officer CW-1 were deleted by this order. Former military clerks, now officers of logistics, received their reversed V shaped chevrons on their rank left sleeve shield patches, the same as were worn by other Czechoslovak officers. Lettering was switched from Russian Cyrillic to the Roman alphabet. Laced left sleeve shield patches were introduced for enlisted men and non-commissioned officers. The color of lacing denoted branch or arm of service (raspberry for rifle

Pavel Šprinc, member of 2nd Cavalry Regiment, picture taken after 21st June 1919. He is wearing a summer variant of the Podyebradka cap made of shipcloth with regular black brush. This cap pattern was invented by members of 2nd Cavalry Regiment and introduced in November 1918 in its winter variant as a cavalry cap for daily use (unlike 1st Cavalry Regiment). The summer variant of Podyebradka cap was introduced in April 1919 for 2nd Cavalry Regiment (and which was never introduced for 1st Cavalry Regiment). There is the so called Joint resistance badge on front of the cap, as was issued to Czechoslovak soldiers from April 1919. Šprinc is dressed in a blouse of uncertain pattern, which does not resemble shape of "officer's jacket" as was introduced in summer 1919. Nevertheless there is a twice carved red left shoulder shield patch laced in white, which was introduced just for the "officers' jacket." There is a single epaulette on his left shoulder. There is a service time insignia on his right sleeve in white as given by regulations (it should be of the same color as the left shoulder shield patch was laced in). There is a red shoulder shield patch laced in white on his left sleeve. *Courtesy of VÚA-VHA*

Sergeant J. Kmodras, member of machinegun company of 4th Czechoslovak Regiment, picture taken after 1920. Sergeant Kmodras is dressed in an overcoat of the so called Vladivostok uniform, which was made of green shipcloth made in Japan. Collar tabs sewn-in in a different way are the most obvious change when compared with an overcoat of Russian pattern. There is a shield patch laced in raspberry color on the left sleeve of Kmodras' overcoat. There is a number "4" (of older Russian pattern) on that left sleeve, a shield patch with rank insignia, and a machinegun badge. His cap is the Mark 1919 pattern, which was introduced along with "officers' jacket" on 21st June 1919. It is interesting that despite this picture being taken a long time after his coming home, a white-red ribbon on the cap is missing. *Author's collection*

regiments and for Shock Battalion, brick red color for artillery, white for cavalry, black for doctors and medical personnel, dark blue for veterinarians and veterinary personnel, orange for logistics etc.). Original Russian collar tabs were removed and new ones were of the same color as those worn on the upper-left sleeve.

Later, in 1920, the shape, size and position of collar tabs were adjusted so the difference from original Russian ones became more apparent. Due to Order No. 117 new insignia denoting the length of service with Czechoslovak Legions was introduced to be worn on the right sleeve. All buttons of foreign armies' insignia had to be replaced or at least stitched by cloth. Uniforms and equipment remained still of Russian origin respective of the appearance from years of Civil War. Only both Czechoslovak cavalry regiments were partial exemption.

The above mentioned Order No. 117 reflected a bunch of previously issued orders, e.g. on uniforms of Czechoslovak cavalry and addressed the issue of homemade insignia flood within hastily developing armed forces. There were some more changes introduced during later periods and the system of left sleeve shield patches was widened (e.g. rank of Chief Warrant Officer CW-1 was deleted without replacement), but those few changes were cosmetic only and we can say that our legionaries returned to their homeland with left sleeve shield patches fully corresponding to the Order No. 117.

The situation with the Czechoslovaks' own uniform was a bit different. Czechoslovak authorities and representatives streamed to create such a uniform since 1914; their effort came into a successful end and new uniform was introduced finally in 1919. Order of Czechoslovak Forces in Russia No. 41 dated 21st June 1919 introduced "service cap Mark 1919" and new officers' blouse named "jacket for officers." That blouse as a part of so called "Vladivostok Uniform" was later issued to all Czechoslovak legionaries in Russia irrespective of their rank. Besides the above mentioned service caps and jackets there were more parts of so-called Vladivostok uniform – trousers, overcoat and boots. These uniforms were made of Japanese cloth, whose characteristic color was khaki, but not only this cloth was used for making new uniforms. Service caps were widely used at first and many legionaries wore them with older uniforms of Russian origin. Officers wore jackets at first. The great majority of enlisted men received their new uniforms in Vladivostok, just before departing for their journey home.

A large quantity of 60,000 new sets of uniforms and boots ordered in Japan did not reach Czechoslovak Legion troops and was issued and used later by the Czechoslovak Army in their homeland.

The description of equipment of non-Russian origin, which was issued to Czechoslovak Legionnaires, is far beyond the content of this book. We should only mention that Czechoslovak legionaries were equipped with pouches for a French Chauchat machinegun, an

Rifleman belonging to recce company of the 5th Czechoslovak Regiment. He is dressed in an "officers' jacket." This fully follows regulations. This jacket was issued to all soldiers of Czechoslovak Armed Forces in Russia regardless of their rank on yet unknown date at the break of 1918/1919. He is wearing a "cap Mark 1919" pattern. There is a number "5" and a green stripe below it on the raspberry left sleeve shield patch laced in white. This denoted regimental intelligence service members. *Author's collection*

Sergeant Václav Havlíček, member of telephone detachment of 8th Czechoslovak Regiment, picture taken in 1920. He is wearing an "officers' jacket." There is signals insignia under his rank chevrons on his left shoulder shield patch with number "8." *Author's collection*

Arisaka rifle of Japanese origin with accessories, and haversacks or mess kits of U.S. Army origin.

Uniforms of Czechoslovak automobile units of 1918-1920 period are not mentioned by orders frequently. There is no mention of armored cars crews uniforms in those orders at all. In such cases we have to rely even more on photographs.

According to Order No. 15, enlisted men and non-commissioned officers received a left sleeve shield patch without galloon, with insignia of automobile units (eventually with insignia of armored car units). Those insignia were stenciled by yellow oil paint. There should be lettering „ЧС" below that insignia stenciled again with yellow oil paint on the tab.

Galloon of raspberry color and insignia or numbers made of metal were issued to officers. color of metal insignia, lettering and numbers were never officially stated or adjusted by orders of Czechoslovak Corps except of an order to one of our two cavalry regiments.

Czechoslovak legionaries of all ranks usually used emblems and numbers made of metal. One single picture was discovered providing evidence of non-metallic insignia (probably a painted one) being worn by a Czechoslovak car crewmember as was mentioned above. When Order No. 117 was issued, the left sleeve shield patch galloon was of raspberry color for enlisted men and officers belonging to Czechoslovak automobile units, for technical staff there was olive green color ordered, black was prescribed for medical personnel and officers (former doctors) and orange was worn on the left sleeve shield patches of administrative staff and officers (former military clerks). An emblem of automobile units remained unchanged. This fact was confirmed by Order No. 117 stating: "specialists insignia are as follows… for mechanicians of automobile detachments – winged wheel with a steering wheel." According to known pictorial evidence all members of Czechoslovak automobile units used such insignia, not only by mechanicians. Original Russian insignia of armored car units' crewmembers has not been mentioned by orders at all. The order introduced Czech "ČS" letters. There should be Roman numbers – e.g. "I," "II" or "III" – worn on the left sleeve shield patches of unit members attached to headquarters or staff of rifle divisions.

The only order discovered yet, which directly deals with uniforms of Czechoslovak automobile service, was Order of Czechoslovak Forces in Russia No. 57 dated 22. August 1919, by which the wearing of leather service caps by automobile company personnel was officially accepted until further notice.

Existing photographs provide evidence that members of Czechoslovak automobile units wore frequently (but not all of them) peaked caps of various shapes made of leather. Some of those caps seem to be original Russian ones as those were officially issued to car drivers, some of those were of a shape very similar to caps of Russian line infantry.

We can see various kinds of different goggles for drivers worn on their caps. There are pictures discovered earlier of soldiers wearing automobile insignia on the flange of a service cap or on the left side of his breast.

Many members of Czechoslovak automobile units wore so called „Swedish jackets" either officially issued or acquired on their own. There are rare pictures of Czechoslovak soldiers wearing trousers made of leather or trousers and jacket made of leather. Members of Czechoslovak automobile units were as equipped as their Russian counterparts were with an officially issued uniform consisting of rubashka, trousers etc.

Russian insignia or emblems for car crews can be seen in the pictures. Some of Czech variants of Russian insignia can be found there, too. This

Second Lieutenant belonging to 1st Czechoslovak Regiment. He is wearing a "cap Mark 1919" pattern, an overcoat made of green Japanese shipcloth from so-called "Vladivostok uniform." *Author's collection*

Major Fajfr, commander of 1st Light Artillery Regiment, 1919. There are regular triangle collar tabs on his "officers' jacket", but it is obvious the owner let the tailor add pockets according to his manner. Collar tabs are made of red color for artillery, the same as the left shoulder shield patch's lace. There are crossed gun barrels and number "1" on the patch. *Courtesy of VÚA-VHA*

Group of members of Czechoslovak automobile unit. We can see at least five so called "Swedish jackets", six different types of goggles for drivers and some leather caps. Soldier sitting in the center has got an emblem of Russian automobile units made of metal on the left sleeve shield patch. Czechoslovak soldiers made that insignia frequently on their own but with proportions a bit changed (lower and wider). *Courtesy of VÚA-VHA*

Drivers of Czechoslovak automobile unit are trying to repair a broken vehicle. Picture taken in Vladivostok, 1919. Driver on the left is wearing so called "Swedish blouse" and a cap, made of leather, driver in the center even has leather trousers. *Courtesy of VÚA-VHA*

Czech variant is lower and wider than the Russian one. A picture of an armored car unit member wearing appropriate Russian insignia has not yet been discovered. Pictures of usual insignia worn by our soldiers are not so rare at all. A picture of a Czechoslovak soldier being accompanied by a Japanese woman has been found, but the insignia is worn on the background of a red triangle pointing up on his left sleeve. Such a triangle used to be an insignia of a Shock Battalion during 1917-1918 period. Maybe that soldier felt himself as a stormtrooper when compared to the rest of car crews.

No more parts of special equipment and clothing for car crews of Russian origin were recognized in available pictures of Czechoslovak legionaries.

FLAGS USED IN THE RUSSIAN CIVIL WAR

Until 1920 the Czechoslovak Republic used the Bohemian white and red flag as the state flag. Here it is shown on the building of Czechoslovak headquarters in Vladivostok. In this state it can clearly be mistaken with the Polish national flag. *Courtesy of VÚA-VHA*

After 1918 Czechoslovak lorries in Russia were marked with red and white symbols. The abbreviation "1. Č. S. A. O." stands for the 1st Czechoslovak Automobile Section. *Courtesy of VHÚ*

An interesting variant of the Czechoslovak flag created by adding coats of arms from Bohemia, Moravia, Silesia and Slovakia to the flag of Bohemia. Czechoslovak Legionnaires used this flag during a parade in New York in 1919. *Courtesy of VÚA-VHA*

The Flag of Bohemia, derived from the colors of a red shield and silver lion from the coat of arms of the Bohemian Kingdom. It was used as the national flag of the Czechs in Bohemia and Moravia in the 19th and 20th centuries. Czechoslovak volunteers used it in 1914-1918 as the state flag. In September 1918 this became the official flag of emerging Czechoslovak State. *Author's collection*

The official flag of the exiled Czechoslovak National Council from September 1918. Between 1919 and 1920 the Czechoslovak Army in Russia used this flag as a Czechoslovak national flag, instead of the previous white over red flag of Bohemia. It was probably a measure to distinguish it from the Polish national flag, which is identical. *Author's collection*

Flag of Czechoslovakia, established by Act No. 252, 15 April 1920. *Author's collection*

At the turn of the 17th and 18th centuries the Russian naval flag was used as a flag denoting business and civil matters. During 1883-1914 it was used as the state flag of the Russian Empire, along with a black-yellow-white flag. It was used unofficially by the Russian Republic in 1917, and during the Russian Civil War also by the Samara KOMUTCH Government, Government of Admiral Kolchak, the Army of South of Russia, and other Russian anti-Bolshevik forces. *Author's collection*

	Russian naval flag used between the early 18th century and October 1917. Russian anti-Bolshevik forces in the Russian Civil War also used it. *Author's collection*
	In 1858 it officially became the State flag of the Russian Empire. It was derived from the black eagle and gold shield emblem of the Russian Tsar. In order to distinguish it from the black-and-gold flag of the Austrian Empire, a white stripe was added. This flag was unpopular in Russia, and, as a result, the Tsar allowed the simultaneous use of the white-blue-red tricolor in 1883. *Author's collection*
	Flag of the Russian Empire, in use from 19th December 1914. After the overthrow of the Tsar in February 1917 it was replaced by a white-blue-red tricolor. *Author's collection*
	After France's defeat by the Prussians at Sedan in 1870, the French Emperor Napoleon III abdicated and the Third French Republic was established. The population of Paris revolted against the new government in March-May 1871. A plain red leaf was taken as the flag of the municipality of Paris at the time of the uprising. This flag is also regarded as a symbol of the international workers' movement. It was also used therefore as the flag of the Russian Bolshevik Party, following the takeover of power in November 1917. *Author's collection*
РСФСР	The flag of the Russian Soviet Federative Republic, used since April 1918 and enacted in the constitution of Soviet Russia in August 1918. Following the establishment of the Soviet Union in 1922, it was pushed into the background as the flag of only one of the union republics. The flag of the USSR took its place and was of similar in appearance, with a hammer and sickle, and a star. *Author's collection*

The Ukrainian People's Republic was proclaimed on 20th November 1917 in Kiev. Its new national flag, in use since 29th December 1917, depicted a blue shield and gold Rurik's trident from the Ukrainian coat of arms. *Author's collection*

The flag of the Ukrainian People's Republic of Workers' and Peasants' Soviets, proclaimed by Russian-oriented Ukrainian Bolsheviks on 25th December 1917 in Kharkov. *Author's collection*

Flag of the Ukrainian Hetmanate, established after a pro-German coup by General Paul Skoropadsky on 29th April 1918 in Kiev. *Author's collection*

The flag of the Ural Interim Government, which was formed in Yekaterinburg on 13th August 1918, after the occupation of the city by Czechoslovaks. *Author's collection*

A later variant of the flag of Ural Interim Government. After the coup by Admiral Kolchak in November 1918, the Government fell apart and its members were executed. *Author's collection*

The flag of the Siberian Autonomous Government in 1917-1918. *Author's collection*

The flag of the Russian Far Eastern Republic, established on 6th April 1920. *Author's collection*

The flag of the Republic of China, used as a civil and commercial flag in the years 1912-1929. Author's collection

The Republic of China maritime flag used from 1913 to 1928. *Author's collection*

Four Fiat-Izhorski armored cars and a Pierce-Arrow heavy armored car of the Russian Shock Regiment on parade by the Siberian Army, 25th April 1919. *Courtesy of VÚA-VHA*

Japanese armored train in Siberia. *Courtesy of VÚA-VHA*

Among the images of unusual armored vehicles brought back by the legionaries to the newly established Czechoslovakia, was this Japanese armored trolley, photographed on the 89th Verst of track at Nikolsk-Ussuriyski. *Courtesy of VÚA-VHA*

Tank mock-up presented during Army Day celebrations in one of the Russian cities, probably in 1919. *Courtesy of VÚA-VHA*

In March 1920, two U.S. Regiments in Siberia strengthened twelve French light tanks: Renault FT 17. One of them, No. 68422, was photographed in front of the Czechoslovak depot at Gnili Ugol in Vladivostok. *Courtesy of VÚA-VHA*

An exotic looking Russian submarine in Vladivostok. *Courtesy of VÚA-VHA*

Celebrating the third anniversary of the Russian February Revolution in Svyetlanskaya Street in Vladivostok, 20th March 1920. In the foreground is an armored car with the number 1 that was one of three produced in the Dalzavod factory in Vladivostok on an American-built Hurlburt truck chassis. *Courtesy of VÚA-VHA*

A detail from the previous picture. An armored car armed with two Maxim machine guns in casemates. *Courtesy of VÚA-VHA*

Armored car No. 1 in Vladivostok – another image from the same place. *Courtesy of VÚA-VHA*

Armored cars in Vladivostok with the numbers 1, 2 and 3 on Svyetlanskaya Street in Vladivostok, 20th March 1920. Vehicle No. 2 was identical to No. 1, while the No. 3 armored car in the background has a machine gun mounted in a revolving turret. Uspensky cathedral temple can be seen at the top left of the picture. *Courtesy of VÚA-VHA*

Armored cars in Vladivostok parade down Svyetlanskaya Street, 20th March 1920. In the foreground can be seen the rear view of armored car No 3 – its rotating turret is clearly visible. *Courtesy of VÚA-VHA*

Armored car No. 1, bogged down in the mud on Poltavskaya Street (now Lazo Street) in Vladivostok after the Japanese coup on 5th April 1920.
Courtesy of VÚA-VHA

CHAPTER 2

CZECHOSLOVAK ARMORED CARS IN ITALY AND SLOVAKIA

Ceremonial assignment of official colors to Czechoslovak Regiments in Rome, Italy 24th May 1918. *Courtesy of VÚA-VHA*

THE ORIGIN OF THE CZECHOSLOVAK LEGION IN ITALY

The Czechoslovak Army abroad emerged during World War I with the help of several states, that fought against the German and Austro-Hungarian Armies. Volunteer units gradually emergedfromin Russia, France and Italy. The Italian legion entered the war under very different circumstances , much later than in Russia or France.

Italy declared war on Austria-Hungary on Wednesday, 24th May 1915. This act ended its neutrality and moved it to the side of the Entente Powers. From 1915 to 1917 the Italian Army acquired a large number of prisoners. Among the Austro-Hungarian soldiers were also conscious defectors from various nationalities who wanted to fight against the old Monarchy alongside Italy and its allies. The Italian government, however, had no understanding of the formation of non-Italian troops. The reasons for this were political and military. Italy sought to obtain power status in the Mediterranean at the expense of Austria-Hungary. Its replacement by new national states would bring complications in the distribution of territorial gains. The

Czechoslovak shock troopers (Arditi) in Italy.
Courtesy of VÚA-VHA

Italian government was also concerned for the fate of Italian prisoners of war, as its politicians expected retaliation from Austro-Hungary. In addition, military strategists feared difficulties arising from language barriers, espionage and desertion. Still, in January 1917, after lengthy negotiations, representatives of the Czechoslovak National Council (ČSNR) managed to separate Czech and Slovak POWs from non-Slavic nationalities of the Austro-Hungarian army in Italian POW camps. The POW camp Santa Maria Capua Vetere was chosen for them. On Monday, 15th January 1917 a society called Czechoslovak Volunteer Corps (ČSDS) was established in this camp. Entrance to this society was permitted to all Czech and Slovak volunteers who were willing to defend the freedom of a nation in arms. In July 1917, Czechoslovak POWs were relocated to a bigger camp in the Certosa di Padula.

Due to the already mentioned distrust of the Italian government to troops from different ethnicities, the option offered to the Czechoslovak Volunteer Force was not utilized. The first Czechoslovak troops (volunteer reconnaissance groups) appeared at the front, on the initiative of frontline commanders and intelligence information departments of the Italian Army, who showed greater responsiveness and military acumen than their government or military superiors. Reconnaissance units consisting of Austro-Hungarian deserters, mostly Czech, Slovak, Croat, Polish and Slovene. For the Italian field Army they were a valuable source of information about the enemy. Czechoslovak recon-naissance groups were created in September 1917, and particularly during March-April 1918. All Italian field armies operating against Austria-Hungary formed such groups. The Italian government changed its attitude towards the creation of a Czechoslovak Army, which happened in late 1917. In the battle for Caporetto on 24th October 1917, the Italian military was defeated and its losses amounted to 430,000 killed, wounded and captured. Starting on Monday 11th February 1918 recruitment to Czechoslovak labor battalions began. These participated in building fortified zone in the rear of the Italian Army around Venice.

On 21st April 1918, however, there was a turning point. Thanks to the diplomatic skills of Milan R. Štefánik, the Czechoslovak National Council managed to sign an agreement with the Italian government about the establishment of Czechoslovak military units in Italy. Accordingly, these units would be part of an independent Czechoslovak Army in France, and were politically subordinate to the Czechoslovak National Council in Paris, although tactically they reported to the Italian Army High Command. This treaty envisaged a higher deployment of military units, if necessary, outside Italy.

Labor battalions were taken as a basis for the organization of the Czechoslovak Corps in Italy (Corpo czecoslovacco in Italia – not to be confused with the Czechoslovak Army Corps – Corpo d'Armata, formed later): on 20th April 1917 these consisted of 7,724 persons. Four rifle regiments were created on the basis of these battalions in the area of Foligno and Perugia. Starting on Tuesday 23rd April 1918, Czechoslovak regiments were brigaded in pairs into the I and II Brigade in the newly established 1st Division of the Czechoslovak Corps Italy (Corpo Czeco Slovacco in Italia – 1a Division). Until now operating independently, Czechoslovak reconnaissance companies were administratively incorporated into the 2nd battalion of 1st Regiment.

The forming of the division took place very quickly. In May 1918, it had 11,840 members and by June 15,680 members. Besides rifle regiments, other units were established as well. Some of them were Italian units, especially artillery. The number of Italian nationals in the Division ranged from 700 to 800 persons. On Friday 24th May 1918, the day of the third anniversary of Italy's entry into the war, in Rome a ceremony was held for the handing over of the division color from the Czechoslovak National Council representative, Colonel Milan R. Štefánik, to the division commander, the Italian General Andrea Graziani. On the basis of a decision of the Czechoslovak National Council in Paris, units and Czechoslovak units in Italy were re-named. According to the order of 1st Division of Czechoslovak Corps in Italy No 22 of 3rd June 1918, its 1st to 4th regiments were re-designated to the 31st to 34th Regiment. Division Order of the Day No 53 of

11th July 1918, ordered the re-naming of 1st Division to the 6th Division and its brigades, which were originally identified by the Roman numerals I and II were renamed into to XI and XII Brigade. The 6th Division left for the front in the middle of August 1918. It was subordinate to the HQ of the Italian 1st Army and deployed in the area between Lago di Garda Lake and Adige River in the area of Altissimo.

Ongoing recruitment of Czech and Slovak volunteers facilitated the expansion of the Army, and compensated for losses and the building of new units, especially the 35th Rifle Regiment. The independently operating reconnaissance companies created the 39th Rifle Regiment, which served as their administrative HQ. The second reorganization took place on 17th November 1918, when 6th Division was extended to the Army Corps of the Czechoslovak Corps in Italy (Corpo czecoslovacco in Italia – Corpo d'Armata) – its brigades were enhanced by adding a third rifle regiment and expanded to a 6th and 7th Division. Additional artillery, cavalry, special and rear units were also created. The newly formed Army Corps consisted of 19,400 persons and six rifle regiments, two artillery regiments, a cavalry group with two squadrons, a heavy artillery section and other corps units. A corps commander, the Italian general Luigi Piccione, was appointed. The commander of the 6th Division was the Italian general Gaston Rossi and Italian general Giuseppe Boriani took over the 7th Division.

On Wednesday 11th December 1918 the Czechoslovak Legion in Italy commenced its return journey to Czechoslovakia. Members of the 39th Regiment were the first to arrive in the newly created Czechoslovak Republic, which also formed part of the personal guard unit for President Tomáš Garrigue Masaryk. Seventy-three trains left Italy – the last on Thursday 26th December 1918. For the needs of the departing Army Corps, about 3,000 railway wagons and a corresponding number of locomotives were earmarked. The transport cargo included 3,000 horses and mules, 300 trucks, plus artillery material and a spare rifle for each soldier. Each individual was fitted with a weeks' emergency ration and three trains contained enough food supplies for twenty-one days for the entire Corps. The Italian government provided this to its Czechoslovak ally.

During the transportation of this cargo through former enemy legionaries were on the alert against possible attack. Some losses were suffered, mainly food supplies. From the historians' perspective, the saddest loss occurred in Wörgl in the Tyrol. Here personal baggage belonging to the divisional photographer Bohumil Dvořák disappeared, along with a rich photographic documentation of the life and struggles of Czechoslovak volunteers in Italy.

Armored cars, Lancia and Bianchi (right), of the Czechoslovak Army in Italy, autumn 1918. The Bianchi armored car was probably camouflaged in Italian green. The only visible marking on this vehicle in Czechoslovak service is a wide white stripe around the turret. *Courtesy of VÚA-VHA*

1918

The tradition of armored cars in Czechoslovakia began with the arrival of two vehicles from Italy. The Italian military administration supplied two armored cars to the Czechoslovak 6th Division at the end of November 1918. Originally there were different types – the first machine was a product of Bianchi and the other was from the Ansaldo-Lancia company. Commander of the Bianchi armored car was Lieutenant Commander František Kolajda and the Lancia armored car was commanded by Lieutenant Jaroslav Hrdina. The crew of each car consisted of four men, including a commander and his deputy.

On 12 November 1918, the Czechoslovak artillery in Italy was formed. From all other units were selected soldiers who had served in artillery in the Austro-Hungarian Army. Both divisions received a field howitzer regiment. Besides them, corps HQ received a section of heavy howitzers, based in Sabbionara. To this section both armored cars were attached to at first.

On 19th November 1918 Army Corps HQ created a cavalry group, composed of the 6th and 7th squadron – one for each division, consisting of 120 cavalrymen. These squadrons

The ceremonial march-past of Czechoslovak Corps in Italy in front of the Italian King Victor Emmanuel III in Padua, 8th December 1918. *Courtesy of VÚA-VHA*

reported directly to divisional headquarters. At the turn of November-December 1918, both armored cars were taken from the artillery and the Bianchi armored car was assigned to 6th cavalry squadron while the Lancia to the 7th cavalry squadron.

On Sunday 8th December 1918, both armored cars participated in a ceremony for the handing over of the regimental colors to the Czechoslovak Divisions in Padua, in front of the Italian King, Vittorio Emmanuele III and the Duke of Turin. Preparations began at about four o'clock that morning. The ceremony began at half past nine in the morning and lasted about two hours. According to Jaroslav Podobský's memoirs, legionaries from the 35th Rifle Regiment took part in a show consisting of, "Czech cavalry on nice horses and two armored cars." Another participant, Frank Bednařík, recalled that, "two armored cars, stood behind the cavalry, making up the whole background of a very picturesque view." J. Podobský's recollections continue: "On one (unarmored) car that came before the main grandstand, near to where we stood, a receiving cinematic apparatus was placed. Then came the signal: Attention! A crowd of officers and some senior figures in civilian clothing appeared on the grandstand. Then someone spoke, and apparently it was Dr. Lev Borský." ... "The end of the parade was a celebration of our troops before the Italian King. Each company went before him separately, platoons in rows of four men. I imagined the Italian King as I saw his picture on Lira paper banknotes, and yet before me I saw a decrepit old man who differed from other senior officers standing around him on account of his stature. "After the speech by Dr Borský the entire Army Corps sang the national anthem. Captain Šeba read the military

General Gaston Rossi, commander of the 6th Czechoslovak Division. *Courtesy of VÚA-VHA*

General Giuseppe Boriani (third from left), commander of the 7th Czechoslovak Division. *Courtesy of VÚA-VHA*

oath, after which all regiments received official colors and then they marched in front of the Italian King. Armored vehicles, heavy and field batteries of artillery and two cavalry squadrons ended the infantry march-past.

A few days later – on 16th and 17th December 1918 – the head of the Czechoslovak exile resistance and president Tomáš Garrigue Masaryk, accompanied by General Piccione, the Commander in Chief of Czechoslovak troops in Italy, inspected Czechoslovak divisions before leaving for home. During his interview with the crews of armored vehicles, T.G. Masaryk asked General Piccione about the types of armored vehicles. Thanks to this intervention a second Lancia replaced the Bianchi armored car.

On Monday 23rd December 1918, both the 6th and 7th squadrons together with their armored cars left with a train from Padua, albeit with a detour via Roveretto, Trento, Bolzano and Vienna to Czechoslovakia. On the way through Austria a state of readiness was declared in the wagons in case of a raid or an attempted of disarmament of the transport vehicles. After crossing the border squadrons continued along the following route: České Velenice, Veselí-Mezimostí, Jindřichův Hradec, Cejl (railway station Cejle-Kostelec), Znojmo, Břeclav and Žilina, to the area Poprad-Velká.

In Poprad armored cars together with their escort separated. The 7th squadron with Lancia No. 2 (the original unchanged car) went towards Galanta

and was assigned to the 7th Infantry Division. The second armored car, Lancia marked with a number 1, stayed until the end of year in Teplice, about 4 km from Poprad, and was assigned to the 6th Infantry Division. There are no records of the operations of these two squadrons during the occupation of Slovakia by the Czechoslovak Army.

On Sunday 29th December 1918, the Czechoslovak Home Army (military units created on Bohemian territory from former officers and ORs of the Austro-Hungarian Army) under the command of Colonel František Schöbl occupied the city of Košice. The Legion from Italy then occupied the first demarcation line between Czechoslovakia and Hungary, which was established by the Pichon Note. On

Padova, Italy, transportation of Czechoslovak legions to their homeland. *Courtesy of VÚA-VHA*

Rail transportation of Czechoslovak Army automobiles from Italy to Czechoslovakia. *Courtesy of VÚA-VHA*

Monday 20th January 1919 an interim border came into existence between Slovakia and the Hungarian Kingdom. It ran along the Danube River up to the Ipel River and then up against Rimavská Sobota; here it left the Ipel and continued in a straight line towards the Uh River, and continued to the old Galician border.

Czechoslovak legionaries from Italy in České Budějovice, Bohemia, winter 1918. Courtesy of *VÚA-VHA*

Malacky, showing the first Czechoslovak flag, officially erected in Slovakia. On the wagon in the foreground is an Austro-Hungarian aircraft (probably an Albatros B.II) is dismantled. *Courtesy of VÚA-VHA*

Supreme Czechoslovak headquarters in Bratislava, Slovakia in the house of Archduke Friedrich. *Courtesy of VÚA-VHA*

1919

The armed forces of the Czechoslovak Republic suffered from a lack of suitable fighting vehicles. Its Army was mostly infantry and was equipped with weapons, which remained in its possession following the disintegration of the Austro-Hungarian Army or weapons which came from abroad together with returning legionaries. General Headquarters solved shortages of armored vehicles by constructing new armored trains, and manufacturing and purchasing armored cars and tanks, although more intensive use was made of both Italian armored cars. The subsequent occupation of Slovakia and skirmishes with troops from the Hungarian Soviet Republic again highlighted the importance for a sufficient number of armored vehicles.

The occupation of the Slovak capital Bratislava took place during the night from 1st to 2nd January by the 7th Division. Its three regiments then marched up to the city of Lučenec. Units of the 6th division occupied the remaining part of the interim border between Lučenec and Užocki Pass. Taking up their positions both divisions passed without significant clashes. The operation ended on Monday, 20th January 1919, when Home Army troops together with legionaries from Italy occupied all of Slovakia up to the first demarcation line. Because the Hungarian-speaking personnel fled, legionaries were obliged to perform tasks such as that of a local gendarmerie and providing security for the provisional borders.

On the first demarcation line, the legionary Bedřich Kuška serving in the 2nd Battalion 34th Rifle Regiment recalls: "The demarcation line was a strange device that kept the battalion HQ staff awake at night, and the more so because it encouraged rebellion in the city. The brothers Chlupáč with Lieutenant Macas detailed on a map a "dig out" and night "hike" where a flash raid occurred on the night of 17th January. He sent us a whole procession of prisoners in the morning and firmly settled in Rapy, Vilka, Litka etc. from where everywhere came Hungarians. But our joy did not last long. After the fall of Balašské Ďarmoty on 29th January, during negotiations on the return of our prisoners of war from the III Battalion, the Hungarians introduced t evacuation of occupied places as their condition. Our headquarters however gave the relevant order to Prchlík too late. His men were attacked by Hungarians on 31st

Cavalry of the 6th Czechoslovak Division in Bratislava. The Lancia has a white stripe on the turret with a black inscription "6. ŠVADRONA" (6th squadron) in the front. *Courtesy of Daniel Minár*

January 1919, part of his company fell into captivity, and eleven were killed."

Italian commanders in the field and other troops soon started experiencing militarily difficulties in sustaining the border and they demanded a second demarcation line, which would include strategically advantageous areas like Novohradsko, Matransko and Bukovsko. The Czechoslovak government asked its delegates at the Paris Peace Conference to seek territorial changes.

After the occupation of Košice by the Czechoslovak Army, the Lancia No. 1 was moved into this city. Used in cases of emergency, and policing, it was also used for the personal protection of General Rossi from Czechoslovak soldiers who suspected him of treason and collaboration with local Hungarians. Surveillance ended after three days.

On Friday 21st March 1919 a temporary Soviet government took power in Hungary and proclaimed the Hungarian Soviet Republic. It held on to power until Friday, 1st August of the same year. After the Communist coup in Hungary, Czechoslovak Minister for Slovakia, Vavro Šrobár, declared martial law in Slovakia on 25th March 1919.

In March Lancia No. 1 went to Rožňava, and then to Rimavská Sobota and Tornala. Their task was to strengthen local military garrisons

General Luigi Piccione, commander of Czechoslovak Corps in Italy, on a visit to Košice, Slovakia. *Courtesy of VÚA-VHA*

Czechoslovak sailors fighting in Slovakia, 1919. *Courtesy of VÚA-VHA*

Automobile column of the 8th Battalion of Czechoslovak Home Guard (Domobrana) from Italy. *Courtesy of VÚA-VHA*

Transportation of Czechoslovak artillery in Slovakia, 1919. *Courtesy of VÚA-VHA*

Czechoslovak armored train "BRATISLAVA" in the station at Slovenský Meděr. *Courtesy of VÚA-VHA*

against an anticipated revolt by local Hungarians. The show of force was successful, and the combat deployment of Lancia No. 1 was not necessary. After a time it was called back to Košice.

By late April the two armored cars were moved by rail to Prague, where they were on standby in case of unrest, which was expected on 1st May. This was followed by a trip to Milovice for sharp shooting practice, before returning to Prague. In Prague Jaroslav Novák, a lieutenant from the Italian legions, took the command of the Lancia No. 2. It returned to Slovakia by rail. Lancia No. 1 was assigned to Nitra and No. 2 continued towards Galanta and Komárno.

THE SECOND DEMARCATION LINE

On Tuesday 29th April, according to general Piccicone's order, Czechoslovak troops moved along a new line, which ran alongside the Novohradské, Matranské and Bukovské mountains up to Miskolc. On the night of 30th April to 1st May units of the 7th Division repelled a Hungarian counter-attack at Komárno. Units of the 6th Division successfully advanced to the southeastern section of the second demarcation line and on 2nd May it occupied the town of Miskolc.

According to the recollections of František Kovanda, a legionary from the 31st Rifle Regiment and signalman of HQ company: "Our first clash was with Hungarian sailors, and our struggle continued to Miskolc. In Serenč, where our dressing station was in the local sugar factory, its owner put his entire house at our disposal. He was a good Czech and had great affection for the legionaries. We were in front of Miskolc. A big offensive was imminent, but I could not participate because I was recalled and assigned as a telephone operator to a Romanian battery. I maintained telephone contact with the Romanian artillery regiment No. 31 and Area HQ. Some day I was at HQ without a telephone connection. A big event was anticipated and the Hungarians blew out our telephone wires. I went with a patrol to repair the lines, despite the fact that the commander of the Romanian battery warned me against this. The Bolsheviks shelled the main road along which our communication line led. We set to work and put everything in order, . However after the line was in order the Bolsheviks surrounded us, although I still managed to put a call through to our Area HQ about the situation in which we found ourselves. We retreated slowly towards Bardějov."

The remaining units of the Czechoslovak Army failed in battles at Salgotarjan. The Hungarian Red Army made use of this opportunity to push the Czechoslovak troops back. On Tuesday 20th May, it conquered Miskolc. The Czechoslovak Army was ordered to retreat to its starting positions, on 22nd and 23rd May.

On Friday 30th May, the Hungarian Red Army on its northern flank launched an attack against the Czechoslovak Army. During this rapid procedure it conquered Lučenec, Rimavská Sobota, Levice, Šahy, Nové Zámky and Košice. On Tuesday 10th June it reached the Polish border. This offensive

Czechoslovak patrol in southern Slovakia, 1919. *Courtesy of VÚA-VHA*

divided the Czechoslovak Army in Slovakia into two parts, the Eastern and Western Group. Backed by the Hungarian Red Army, the Slovak Soviet Republic was proclaimed in Prešov on 16th June 1919. Despite the hopes of Hungarians and Slovak communists, who dreamed that this area would keep up "great offensive" of Russian Red Army, the Slovak Soviet Republic, lasted only three weeks, until Monday 7th July 1919.

During the fighting Italian officers left the 6th and 7th divisions on 31st May and were replaced with French and Czechoslovak officers. The French General Alphonse Rémy Chabord assumed command of the 6th Division and General Louis Hubert Charles Schuhler took charge of the 7h Division.

Map of operations in Slovakia, 1919. *Hana Rozmanitá, courtesy of ČSOL*

STRUGGLE FOR ŠARKÁN - NANA

At the beginning of June, the Lancia No. 1 traveled to Nové Zámky, before moving through Bajč, Perbeta, Nová Víska and Šarkán and on to Nana, which is located on the outskirts of the city of Parkáň. The Czechoslovak defensive line ran in front of the local train station, but the city was occupied at the time by Hungarian troops. The Lancia No. 1 participated in a counterattack, and after an hour of fighting Parkáň was recaptured. The enemy suffered losses, both dead and wounded. Ammunition vehicles were captured as well. During the night Hungarian boats floated up to the bridge occupied by the Czechoslovak Army. On the following day the fight continued. The Hungarians fired from machine guns across the River Danube from Ostrihom's city citadel and also from the river. During the second night the Lancia No. 1 took part in patrols along the road between the town and the railway station. Under cover of darkness the enemy pushed the Czechoslovak troops back-the troops retreated using an armored train. The only possible retreat route for the Lancia was along the road towards the railway station. Part of this road was under fire from Ostrihom's citadel and river monitors, but the armored car escaped. The Lancia surprised the Hungarian crew of the

Artillery in battle with the Hungarian Red Army. *Courtesy of VÚA-VHA*

Hungarian Red Army in Slovakia, 1919. *Courtesy of VHÚ*

Armored train belonging to the Hungarian Soviet Republic. *Courtesy of VHÚ*

Hungarian Red Army enters Košice. *Courtesy of VHÚ*

Czechoslovak armored train destroyed at Nové Zámky. *Courtesy of VÚA-VHA*

armored train. The Lancia's machine guns attacked enemy troops assembled there, as well as those deployed at the railway station and on the road towards Mužla. The Hungarian armored train returned Czechoslovak fire, but its guns missed the target. Near the village of Mužla, during the night, the armored car arrived in Nové Zámky. Later it traveled to Nitra with a message and at the time of its return Nové Zámky had already been occupied by the enemy. The following day the Lancia broke into Nové Zámky under the command of a French officer. The operation was however halted because the commanding officer believed that mines had been fresh planted along the road. mines.

The idea of "the beginning of June" in the introduction to this chapter can be interpreted in two ways: first, it could denote 1st June 1919 and the struggle for Parkan, when the Hungarians deployed gunboats, a Szamos monitor and Fogas patrol boat. According to Hungarian sources, both ships fired on legionary batteries at Parkánynána. Only one of these ships had artillery armament. The Fogas patrol boat lost her cannon in November 1918 during demobilization of Austro-Hungarian fleet. During the rapid rearmament undertaken in Hungary it only had machine guns. Support came from the Szamos, whose crew belonged to the Hungarian Red Fleet. This ship was disarmed in November 1918, but during its reactivation it had received two 10-cm howitzers M 1914, d/19, a Škoda system, two 8-cm guns M 1918, d/30, a Böhler system and three machine guns.

Second, "the beginning of June" may also refer to Saturday 7th June 1919, when Nové Zámky was re-occupied by the Czechoslovak Army. It is likely that the Lancia No. 1 advanced with a group led by the French Major Bonnean, in the direction of Bajč and Perbete. On Tuesday 10th June the Lancia arrived in the village of Strekov. It was only at this point that the armored car led an assault on Parkan via Nová Víska and Šarkán to the village of Nana. During this event, however, the Hungarians had in this area only unprotected and improvised armed civilian vessels. Later, during the second Hungarian attack on Levice, the Major Bonneane group prevented enemy reinforcements from Parkán. However, the advancing Hungarians pushed the Bonneane group back to Nové Zámky on Wednesday 18th June 1919.

Lancia armored car in Komárno. *Courtesy of VÚA-VHA*

Czechoslovak heavy artillery shelling Hungarian positions. *Courtesy of VÚA-VHA*

FIGHT FOR VRÁBLE

From Nové Zámky the Lancia No. 1 went via Nitra to Vráble, which was also occupied by Hungarian troops. In front of the Vráble train station, near the road on which the Lancia arrived, stood an enemy improvised armored train, which forced the Lancia's crew to wait by hiding on a hill in the local vineyards. After 5 p.m. the Hungarian armored train left in the direction of Šurany, and the Czechoslovak armored car moved into the town to support an attack of a company of Czechoslovak sailors. The next day in the afternoon, during a Hungarian counterattack, the Lancia covered retreat of the sailors with machine gun fire. The day after the armored car was called back to brigade HQ in Zlaté Moravce, and was sent through Gartce and Svatý Benedikt to Kozárovce. Here again the car covered a retreat of Czechoslovak troops to Svatý Benedikt. During the evening several Hungarian soldiers attacked the Lancia No. 1 with hand grenades at Kozárovce. This action forced the armored car to retreat to Svatý Benedict. When Levice was taken a few days later, the Lancia carried out a raid on the Velká Kálnica road. It was then assigned as support to a battalion in Dekeneši. This vehicle participated in the destruction of a machine gun nest at Hill 165, near the road from Velká Kálnica to Dolní Varad. After the expulsion of the enemy the battalion captured two horse-drawn wagons, two machine guns and several prisoners. Later the armored car was assigned to a brigade fighting in the direction of Vráble. Here, it carried out reconnaissance in the direction of Nevižany and suffered several bullet hits to the tires. This damage and the lack of a spare tire led to the creation of an improvised machine-gun car on an armored train. The Lancia was placed on a flat car and used in a sortie in the direction of Zlaté Moravce. On 23rd June the improvised armored train carried out an assault on the railway track from the river Žitava in the direction of Fedýmeš, Ohaj, Hul and Rendva. The train crew consisted of two platoons of Czechoslovak legionaries from Italy.

Following the armistice Lancia No. 1 was sent to Prague for repair in the Breitfeld-Daněk factory. As a result, its original tires were replaced with solid rubber tires. Its commander was demobilized and was succeeded by Lieutenant Adolf Prchlík from the Italian (Czechoslovak) legion.

The crewmembers from the Lancia No. 1 were designated for combat in Slovakia with the Czechoslovak War Cross and were mentioned in a divisional order. In August 1919 the repaired armored car Lancia No. 1 went back to Slovakia and was stationed in Kremnica, Ružomberok and Bratislava. In December 1919 its permanent garrison became Lučenec. On 26th October 1919 Lieutenant Karel Janoušek, a legionary from Italy, assumed command of the Lancia No. 2 from Lieutenant Jaroslav Novák. Both Lancia armored cars later served in the Czechoslovak Army. They were withdrawn in December 1936.

Lancia No. 1 in Lučenec, 7th March 1920. *Courtesy of VHÚ and Daniel Minár*

Lancia No. 1 has an accident in Košice on 21st September 1921. A police number, N-VII-751, can clearly be seen on the rear of the car. *Courtesy of VHÚ*

ARMORED CARS FIAT – TORINO

At the end of 1919, after finalizing its battle with the Red Hungarians, the Czechoslovak military began to consider the possibility of manufacturing new armored cars. The impetus for this step came from military commanders in Slovakia. During the last days of December, a prototype of an armored car developed on the chassis of Italian company Fabbrica Italiana Automobili Torino (FIAT) truck was built in the Pilsen Škoda factory. It was introduced to the Czechoslovak Military Commission on 20th January 1920.

The double-turreted armored vehicle was armed with two machine-guns, but it had a weak engine, was slow on the road and was almost incapable of driving on light terrain. Despite this, twelve vehicles were ordered. The manufacture of the body armor and the remaining eleven vehicles was completed in June 1920. These vehicles were taken over directly by several units. However, when on duty, the Fiat-Torino armored cars carried out their tasks with difficulties. These lines refute rumors of deployment of these machines in war against the Hungarian Soviet Republic in 1919.

DEPLOYMENT OF VEHICLES, 1920

Armored car No	Garrison
1	Lučenec
2	Praha
3 and 4	Košice
5 and 6	Bratislava
7 and 8	Opava
9 and 10	Praha
11 and 12	Užhorod
13 and 14	Praha

Armored car Fiat Torino No. 5 and Lancia No. 2. Both vehicles already have police numbers: N-VII-755 or N-VII-752. *Courtesy of VÚA-VHA*

CAMOUFLAGE AND MARKING

The Lancia armored cars in Czechoslovak service probably maintained their original colors – Italian green or a dark brown shade of green. From 1918 to the 1920s, the upper half of the bigger turret was painted with a white stripe. A white framed number appeared on both sides of the vehicle. These vehicles, when in service with the Czechoslovak Army, were painted with a standard green (khaki) color. Police registration numbers, used on Lancia vehicles until November 1932, appeared in white on a black table. Military registration numbers, which replaced police numbers from December 1932 onwards, were white on a black table with a white rim.

Lancia No. 2. Czechoslovak Lancias remained in their original Italian green. Around the bottom of the turret they carried a white stripe. The number of the vehicle was painted in white in a white rectangle on the side. The front and rear bore a black table with a white police number. *Courtesy of Difrologický Club*

Vehicle	Original military evidence number	Police evidence number up to 1932	Military evidence number from December 1932
Lancia	1	N-VII-751	14.023
Lancia	2	N-VII-752	14.024
Fiat-Torino	3 až 14	N-VII-753 až 764	not on strength

Training attack of a Lancia and two Škoda PA-I armored cars in the 1920s. *Courtesy of Difrologický Club*

Rest during training in the 1920s. Note the distinct types of armored cars: Škoda PA-I, Lancia IZ, Škoda PA-I, a prototype Škoda Praga L, and two Fiats Torino. The presence of the Škoda Praga L prototype means the picture can be dated to 1922-1925. *Courtesy of Difrologický Club*

A similar scene as the previous picture, but probably in another place. Lancia's crew is changing a tire. *Courtesy of Difrologický Club*

Convoy of Czechoslovak Army vehicles in the 1920s. This time two Fiat Torino armored cars are leading, followed by a prototype Škoda L-Praga, Škoda PA-I, Lancia IZ and a second Škoda PA-I. *Courtesy of Difrologický Club*

An accident of Lancia No. 2. On the right in the background the armored cars Škoda PA-I and PA-II are visible. *Courtesy of Difrologický Club*

The same Lancia, as in the previous picture. The armored cars Škoda PA-I and PA-III can be seen in the background. *Courtesy of Difrologický Club*

A third view of the overturned Lancia IZ No. 2. *Courtesy of Difrologický Club*

CZECHOSLOVAK ARMORED CARS IN WORLD WAR I AND THE RUSSIAN CIVIL WAR

Probably the same Lancia No. 2, as on the previous three pictures. *Courtesy of Difrologický Club*

Lancia armored cars and a Škoda PA-III on military parade in Milovice in the 1920s. *Courtesy of Karel Straka*

One of the Czechoslovak Lancia armored cars was used as a Russian Legion armored car in Svatopluk Innemann's film "Třetí rota" ("The Third Company"). Shown here is a snapshot from the filming in Milovice, 31st July 1931. *Courtesy of VÚA-VHA*

BIOGRAPHIES

Dvořák, Josef Deputy commander of armored car No. 1, technical sergeant of the Czechoslovak Legion in Italy and Slovakia in 1919, 6th cavalry squadron.

Hrdina, Jaroslav Commander of armored car No. 2, lieutenant of the Czechoslovak Legion in Italy and Slovakia in 1919, 7th cavalry squadron.

Janoušek, Karel Commander of armored car No. 2 from 26th October 1919, lieutenant of the Czechoslovak Legion in Italy and Slovakia in 1919, 7th cavalry squadron.

Kolajda, František (Kolojda ?) Commander of armored car No. 1, probably until October 1919, lieutenant of the Czechoslovak Legion in Italy and Slovakia in 1919, 6th cavalry squadron.

Novák, Jaroslav Commander of armored car No. 2 from May 1919 to 26th October 1919, lieutenant of the Czechoslovak Legion in Italy and Slovakia in 1919, 7th cavalry squadron.

Prchlík, Adolf Commander of armored car No. 1 probably from October 1919, lieutenant of Czechoslovak legion in Italy and Slovakia in 1919, 6th cavalry squadron.

GEOGRAPHICAL NAMES IN ITALY

Czech:	Italian:
Benátky	Venezia
Gardské jezero	Lago di Garda
Adiže, řeka	Adige
Padova	Padua, or Padova
Trident	Trento

GEOGRAPHICAL NAMES IN SLOVAKIA AND HUNGARY

Czech	Hungarian:	German:	Slovak:	Note:
Bajč	Bajcs		22nd April 1920	
Balašské Ďarmoty	Balassagyarmat			Now in Hungary
Bardějov	Bárdfa, or Bártfa	Bartfeld	Bardejov	
Bratislava	Pozsóny	Pressburg	Prešpurk,	
now Bratislava	Josef	20th January 1920	4th February 1920	
Bukovsko, Mountains	Bükk			Now in Hungary
Dekeneš	Kysgyékénes		Rohožnica,	
now Veľký Ďur	Vladimír	20th January 1920	22nd April 1920	Section Commander
Děvín	Devény	Theben	Devín	also mentioned as Kneisl
Dolní Varád	Alsóvárad		Dolný Varád, now	

Czech	Hungarian:	German:	Slovak:	Note:
Tekovský Hrádok	František	20th January 1920	22nd April 1920	
Dunaj, River	Duna	Donau	Dunaj	also mentioned as Pýcha
Fedýmeš	Zsitvafődémes		Fedýmeš nad	also mentioned as Pilsker
Žitavou, now	Alfons	20th January 1920	22nd April 1920	
Úľany nad Žitavou	Karel			
Galanta	Galánta		Galanta	also mentioned as Schubert
Gartce	Garamnémeti		Nemce, now	
Tekovské Nemce	Josef	20th January 1920	22nd April 1920	also mentioned as Velikovský
Halič		Galizien		Polish Halicz,
Ukrainian Halyčina	Karel	20th January 1920	22nd April 1920	
Hul	Hul		Hul	
Humenné	Homonna		Humenné	
Ipl, River	Ipoly		Ipeľ	
Komárno	Komárom	Komorn	Komárno	
Košice	Kassa	Kaschau	Košice	
Kozárovce	Garamkovácsi		Kozárovce	
Kremnice	Körmöcbánya	Kremnitz	Kremnica	
Krompachy	Korompa	Krompach	Krompachy	
Levice	Léva		Levice	
Litka	Litka			Now in Hungary
Lučenec	Losonc		Lučenec	
Matransko, Mountains	Mátra			Now in Hungary
Michalovce	Nagymihály		Michalovce	
Miškovec	Miskolc			Now in Hungary

Czech	Hungarian:	German:	Slovak:	Note:
Mužla	Muzsla		Mužla	
Nana	Parkánynána, or			
Esztergomnána		Nána, now Štúrovo		
Nevižany	Nevéd		Nevidzany	
Nitra	Nyitra	Neutra	Nitra	
Nová Víska	Kisújfala		Nová Vieska	
Nové Zámky	Érsekújvár	Neuhäusel	Nové Zámky	
Novohradsko, Mountains	Börzsöny			Now in Hungary
Ohaj	Ohaj		Dolný Ohaj	
Parkáň	Parkány		Parkán,	
now Štúrovo				
Perbeta	Perbete		Perbeta,	
now Pribeta				
Poprad	Poprád	Deutschendorf	Poprad	
Rapy	Rapy			Now in Hungary
Rendva	Rendve		Radava	
Rimavská Sobota	Rimaszombat		Rimavská Sobota	
Rožňava	Rozsnyó	Rosenau	Rožňava	
Růžomberk	Rózsahegy	Rosenberg	Ružomberok	
Sabinov	Kisszeben	Zyben	Sabinov	
Salgótarján	Salgótarján			Now in Hungary
Serenč	Szerencs			Now in Hungary
Svatý Benedikt	Garamszentbenedek		Svätý Beňadik, now	
Hronský Beňadik				
Šahy na Iplu	Ipolyság		Šahy	
Šarkán	Sárkányfalva		Šarkan	

Czech	Hungarian:	German:	Slovak:	Note:
Šurany,	Nagy Surány		Veľké Šurany,	
now Šurany				
Teplice	Szepestapolcza		Teplica, now	
Spišská Teplica				
Tornala	Tornalja		Tornaľa,	
ex Šafárikovo				
Už or Uh, River	Ung		Uh	
Velká Kalnice	Nagy Kálna		Veľká Kálnica, now	
Kalná nad Hronom				
Velká				
u Popradu	Felka		Veľká, now Poprad	
Verovce				
u Dunaje	Verőce			Now in Hungary
Vilka	Vilka			Now in Hungary
Vráble	Verebély		Vráble	
Zlaté Moravce	Aranyosmárot		Zlaté Moravce	
Žilina	Zsolna	Silein	Žilina	
Žitava, River	Zsitva		Žitava	

UNIFORMS OF ARMORED CAR CREWS BELONGING TO CZECHOSLOVAK LEGIONS IN ITALY

Czechoslovak legionaries in Italy in 1918, and later during the fighting for Slovakia in 1919, were issued with uniforms and equipment corresponding to regulations of Italian armed forces except for national insignia, rank and arm of service or branch insignia. Those insignia elements particularly underlined the autonomy of Czechoslovak Corps. Hats, typical headgear of Alpini, Italian mountain infantry, were worn by enlisted men and by officers as was accepted by the Order of Czechoslovak Corps in Italy – I. Czechoslovak Division No. 17 dated 16. May 1918. Vertical bicolor white-red ribbon was pinned to and worn as a national insignia on the front of hats, some intelligence gathering companies used oval cockade of the same colors made

Subcommittee of Czechoslovak prisoners of war society – Czechoslovak Volunteer Corps, Padula, April 1918. Prisoners were allowed to wear Italian uniforms and national insignia (red-white ribbons and armbands). At the same time they were permitted to use insignia of their former Austro-Hungarian ranks. Their insignia was derived from an Italian one and later, until 1918, it was used as enlisted men and non-commissioned officers insignia of Czechoslovak Legions in Italy. We can see prisoners of war with rank of Corporal (caporale) – one man and two Sergeants (caporale maggiore). *Author's collection*

A group of Czechoslovak mortarmen, picture taken before 29th November 1918. A man standing to the right of the officer sitting on the chair in the center has rank insignia of Corporal on his left sleeve. There are probably mortar badges of Italian origin and Czechoslovak left sleeve shield patches with "ČS" letters sewn-in purple and a number of the regiment. The officer sitting on the chair has vertical rank insignia. Legionaries have got Alpini hats, which were introduced in Czechoslovak regiments on 16th May 1918. There is a black falcon badge with white-red cockade on the falcon's chest. The date when this badge was introduced is still unknown. *Courtesy of VÚA-VHA*

Legionaries, a member of 33rd Czechoslovak Rifle Regiment – picture probably taken before 29th November 1918. He is wearing an Alpini hat with black falcon badge and white-red cockade on its chest. The regimental number made of metal was worn frequently in the center of cap badge as is shown here. The legionary is wearing a regular Italian jacket with Czechoslovak collar tabs – white-red on blue background. There is no metal badge or insignia on these tabs, as such insignia were introduced on 29th November 1918. No five pointed stars made of metal are shown on the tabs either – Italian enlisted men and officers wore those exclusively. There is a Czechoslovak left sleeve shield patch with sewn-in letters, "ČS" in purple and the number of the regiment on the left sleeve. *Courtesy of VÚA-VHA*

Second Lieutenant (sottotenente) of the 35th Czechoslovak Rifle Regiment – picture taken before 29th November 1918. A black falcon badge is missing on front of his Alpini hat, as the badge was introduced later. Instead, there is a sewn-in Czechoslovak shield – a red shield with silver two-tailed lion. The legionary is wearing an Italian officers' jacket. There is a shield patch on the left sleeve with sewn-in letters "ČS" in silver and the number "35." The sleeve cuffs are interesting – Czechoslovak officers were not allowed to wear any Italian rank insignia (stars). Instead, double stripes (originally denoting rank of Italian officers on their caps) were worn in appropriate numbers. *Author's collection*

Rifleman (fuciliere) of an unknown Czechoslovak Rifle Regiment – picture taken after 29th November 1918. There is a colored pompon on the left side of his Alpini hat, denoting that he belongs to a particular battalion within regiment or to brigade or divisional machinegun company. Legionaries used to put a falcon's feather under the so called joint badge of resistance made of metal on the pompon. Metal insignia can be seen on the tabs – crossed rifles which were introduced after 29th November 1918. Different insignia (machineguns, crossed artillery barrels, postal trumpet etc.) were used for the different arms of service and branches. *Author's collection*

Rifleman belonging to an unknown Czechoslovak Rifle Regiment, assault soldier (Arditi) – picture taken after 29th November 1918. There is an Italian Arditi badge below the Czechoslovak shield patch on his left sleeve. *Author's collection*

This group of Arditi belongs to the 33rd Czechoslovak Rifle Regiment – picture taken after 29th November 1918. They are wearing Italian Arditi uniforms including jackets with open collars, and black caps with tassels. Along with the Czechoslovak shield patch on the left sleeve, there are appropriate Italian Arditi badges (for enlisted men and for officers) worn on the left sleeve of their uniforms. One of soldiers in the center of picture even has a badge in the shape of light Hussites' chalice. Some Czechoslovak rank insignia is visible there, those were introduced on 29th November 1918 in Italy. Thse consisted of horizontal rank stripes, purple, purple woven stripes, silver, gold, and special rank insignia for generals. The soldier, mentioned above, wearing a badge of Hussites' chalice has the three stripes of a Staff Sergeant. All Czechoslovak Arditi in the picture wear white-red collar tabs adjusted to the shape of Arditi collar tabs. *Courtesy of VÚA-VHA*

of cloth. Later there was a black falcon sewn on hats of some Czechoslovak legionaries bearing a bisected cockade with white and red fields. There was a single colored pompon fixing a quill on the left side of the hat worn in the Italian style as was accepted by the above mentioned order. The color of that denoted battalion in the regiment – white for first battalion, red one for second battalion, green one for third battalion and blue color for brigade and divisional machinegun companies. Some of Italian officers wore those holders in a form of cockade with a cross made of metal and with laces denoting particular rank. There was a rank insignia in the shape of a reversed V around the pompon.

Italian officers used to wear the caps of Italian infantry, again with appropriate rank insignia. Enlisted men were issued with jacket and trousers made of grey-green (grigio – verde) cloth Mark 1909. The jacket was made without pockets but with covered buttons and sewn in V shaped inserts on outer edges of shoulders (this was similar to rolls sewn in the shoulder

Two Czechoslovak Arditi, Second Lieutenants. There are white-red tabs on the collars of their uniforms – adjusted to the shape of Arditi collar tabs – and black flames. Assault soldier on the right is wearing a badge of Arditi officers. There are combat knives – pugnale – visible on their belts. *Courtesy of VÚA-VHA*

Lieutenant-General Luigi Piccione. The rank insignia of Czechoslovak Italian Legions general, as was introduced on 29th November 1918, is clearly seen on his cap and sleeve. Worn on both the cap and sleeve, it is quite visible in the picture. A red stripe with golden lime leaves on the cap and two plus two golden stripes on sleeves of uniform form the full rank insignia. The red stripe is interrupted by the space for two sewn-in, six pointed, golden stars. Similar insignia is worn on the Italian infantry cap. Two-tailed lions are sewn-in gold on the collar of uniform. According to regulations, there should also be stars in front of the lion insignia, but General Piccione wears only one Italian five-pointed star which has nothing to do with his rank. *Courtesy of VÚA-VHA*

Lieutenant-General Piccione with an Italian Major General in Bratislava. Their rank insignia for Czechoslovak Italian Legions is clearly visible, as well as differences between their ranks. *Courtesy of VÚA-VHA*

edge of Austro-Hungarian uniform jackets and later Czechoslovak uniforms which were there to hold weapon straps and equipment carriers and not let them to fall down from the shoulder). There were epaulettes with company number within the regiment sewn in white to black square in an Italian manner. Some of the soldiers bought their own jackets of military shape but with pockets. Officers were issued the Mark 1909 variant of uniform, made of cloth of very same color as for enlisted men but with four pockets. Legionaries wore the raincoat instead of overcoat, the so called mantelini. Enlisted men were equipped with belt and ammunition pouches. Webbing straps around the soldier's neck carried the belt but those straps were fixed only on ammunition pouches. Grey-green puttees and boots were also part of the uniform. Legionaries were issued an Italian modification of the Adrian helmet marked as M 16, on which sometimes appeared a red oval with Czech lion on front of its shell.

Czechoslovak legionary in Italy, a warrant officer with special benefits – picture probably taken on 6th June 1920, Rychnov nad Kněžnou, Czechoslovakia. The rank insignia on the sleeves is very interesting, as it consists of two woven purple stripes. The uniform jacket was heavily tailored. Such habit was typical for Italian legionaries from 1919 and later. *Author's collection*

Group of Czechoslovak legionaries and soldiers. They wear rank insignia as introduced on 29th November 1918 including insignia of frontline service below the left sleeve shield patch, and machinegun units' insignia on white-red tabs. The jackets of these servicemen were obviously heavily tailored and the shape is far beyond regulation limits. *Author's collection*

Collar tabs were fixed to the stand up collar of the jacket where arm of service or branch tabs along with infantry brigade insignia were carried by Italian soldiers. Instead of those, only white-red square tabs in Czechoslovak national colors on blue background were worn by legionaries on the stand up collar. Some Italian soldiers and officers, when attached to our units, continued to wear the insignia of their former units or the so called Savoy star (insignia reserved exclusively to Italian soldiers) on the collar tabs of the national colors. There is a picture of a 6th Czechoslovak Division doctor, Luigi Virgili, who wears red-purple tab of medical personnel on a white-red collar tab and certainly his Savoy star, too. On the left sleeve there was regimental insignia worn by legionaries who did not obey Italian regulations. Such insignia was worn in the form of a square of grey-green cloth with sewn-in number of regiment – from time to time only a small shield patch was worn on the sleeve with a black sewn-in number. There was a sleeve shield patch introduced later the very same size as worn in Russia, and made of grey-green cloth with printed (in purple color for enlisted men) or sewn in purls (in white for officers) lettering ČS with regimental number below. Also worn were specialization insignia on the left only or on both sleeves by some legionaries according to Italian regulations. One of these insignia patches was designed for automobile

machinegunners. Rank insignia was worn on both sleeve cuffs by non-commissioned officers and officers. At the very beginning, members of intelligence companies and labor battalions used to wear Italian rank insignia to denote Czechoslovak ranks, with the exception of using direct stripes sewn-in diagonally from bottom left to top right instead of the reversed V shaped Italian chevrons. Rank insignia for Czechoslovak officers was the same as Italian. Some Czechoslovak intelligence companies introduced their own Czechoslovak rank insignia system. Independent and unique Czechoslovak rank insignia system was created when first labor battalions were formed. It consisted of vertical stripes denoting rank even after the formation of the Czechoslovak division. When the division was raised to army corps level, some changes appeared in that system. These changes were introduced by permanent order No. 500 of the Czechoslovak Depot (reserve unit) located in Foligno and dated 29th November 1918 – it refers to the previously issued Order No. 3736 of Czechoslovak Corps Headquarters dated 23rd November 1918. This order introduced the Alpini hat to be worn by all Czechoslovak and Italian personnel – both enlisted men and officers except of generals with permission for Italian officers to wear the Italian infantry cap during off service time. The same order states that a special tab with badges of Czechoslovak lands must be used to fix

the quill on the left side of the Alpini hat. These badges of Czechoslovak Lands were called the joint badges of resistance. The quill should be of an eagle, grey for enlisted men and junior officers, white for senior officers. Around the quill there was a reversed V shaped Italian rank insignia. The falcon badge on front of the Alpini hat was made of black wool for enlisted men and black silk for officers. This order introduced the arm of service and branch insignia made of metal – oxidized for enlisted men, silver for junior officers, and gold for senior officers – which should be sewn to the front portion of white-red collar tab on a blue background square. There was no special insignia for armored car crews mentioned in the order, unfortunately. The tab on the left lower sleeve remained in use, but only for those servicemen, who joined Corps before the armistice on the Italian front on 4th November 1918. There could be one additional insignia worn below the tab on the left lower sleeve denoting service with other Allied armed forces by silver V shaped chevrons for every six months of service – insignia to be positioned as mentioned above. There were insignia issued for being wounded, and a stripe for special war effort within the Czechoslovak Corps. Rank insignia were changed and vertical rank stripes were switched to horizontal types (vertical types were for newly formed home defense units) in purple color for enlisted men, purple wavy for non-commissioned officers, silver for junior officers, and gold for senior officers. Special insignia in the form of gold embroidered lime leaves on the background of red stripe with golden laces was used for generals. Such insignia should be worn around both sleeves and around the Italian generals' cap – number of stripes equals the rank of general. There was either nothing or gold stars (one or two of them) sewn into that stripe, again according to rank. There are pictures of Czechoslovak Army Corps commander General Piccione, along with another general – probably one of division commanders – wearing that uniform. With the aim to keep the homeland forces informed, this information was listed in the Ministry of National Defense Journal, Issue II, dated 1st April 1919, part 6 factual, article 138. This rank system was put under further development in the process of a gradual unification of ranks of Legions and Armed Forces in the homeland.

CHAPTER 3

ARMORED CARS USED BY THE CZECHOSLOVAK LEGION

Austin armored car, first series. *Courtesy of VHÚ*

Austin armored car, third series. *Courtesy of VHÚ*

AUSTIN

After the outbreak of war in 1914, the government of the Russian Tsar ordered a large number of armored cars from all over allied Europe. In September 1914, the Austin Motor Co. Ltd., in Birmingham, England, received technical specifications from the Russians. The company strengthened chassis of its "Colonial" truck, provided it with a powerful engine (with an estimated 30 horsepower) and built armored superstructure according Russian project. A prototype of the new armored car was ready for serial production in October. By the end of the year, Austin had produced the first series of forty-eight vehicles, several of which arrived in St Petersburg in December 1914. Thse formed the basis of Russia's independent automotive machine-gun platoons. Following combat experience in the field, the prototype was slightly modified. Sixty machines from a second series were shorter in length and had a slightly different cab roof. These vehicles started arriving in Russia by mid-1915. The Austin Company manufactured the last set of vehicles, ordered by the Tsar in a third batch, at the end of 1916. Compared with the previous series, they were different, yet again, and underwent more modifications, namely they had an even more powerful engine of 50 horsepower, dual control, twin wheels on the rear axle and improved armor protection. After the October Bolshevik Revolution in 1917, however, these orders were cancelled and the last forty machines ready for shipment in Birmingham were acquired by the British Army.

Apart from these armored cars, the Russia government also purchased sixty unarmored Austin chassis. In September 1917 the Putilov Plant in St Petersburg received the chassis. In 1919-1920 the plant built thirty-three armored superstructures with distinctive diagonally placed turrets. Twenty-one of them was placed on Austin chassis, and twelve of these superstructures were put on Austin-Kegresse half-track chassis.

During the war, numerous Austin armored cars were rebuilt in field workshops in Russia. In many cases the armored hull of these cars were transferred to other chassis, such as White, Fiat and Packard. However, by combining parts from the Austin first and second series, a unique single-turreted Austin emerged.

The Russian Army on the Eastern Front in World War I extensively deployed Austin armored cars. Both original Austin and Austin-Putilov armored cars almost all sides during the

Russian Civil War extensively deployed as well. During 1918-20, in addition to the Red and White Armies, they were also used by Ukrainians, Germans, Austrians, Lithuanians, Poles and Japanese. In addition, the Czechoslovak Legion also captured an unknown number of these machines. Two of them – an Austin third series and a unique single-turreted Austin first/second series – remained in service with the Czechoslovak Legion until 1920. Starting in 1918, the British Army used Austin armored cars in the Middle East, Ireland and India.

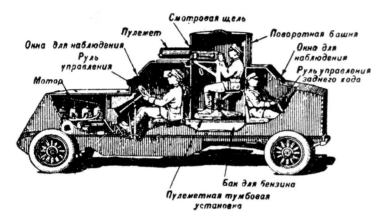

A historical Russian cut-away of an Austin third series armored car. The driving place for the reverse movement is clearly visible. The petrol tank is in the best-protected place of the machine, under the turret. *Courtesy of VHÚ*

BASIC TECHNICAL DATA (ESTIMATED): Austin third series

Crew	5	
Weight	5,3t	
Length	475cm	
Width	190-200cm	
Height	245cm	
Headroom	22cm	
Wheel base	350cm	
Turret	2	
Tires	920x120	
Performance	Engine	gasoline, 50 HP
	Maximum speed	50 km/h
	Range	250 km
Armor	Front	4-5 mm
	Sides	4-5 mm
	Bottom and roof	4,5 mm
	Turrets	4,5 mm
Armament	2x machine-gun Maxim 1910 caliber 7,62 mm	
	Munitions carried	6000 pieces

Replica of the single turreted Austin first/second series built by Jan Queisner in 2010. *Courtesy of Jiří Charfreitag*

ARMSTRONG-WHITWORTH-FIAT, ARMSTRONG-WHITWORTH-JARROT

In early 1915, the Russian Army ordered forty armored cars from Armstrong-Whitworth Co. Ltd. Stockwoods Works in Tyneside, UK. The armored hull was supplied by Vickers Company: the first ten machines were manufactured on chassis' supplied by the Charles Jarrot and Letts truck company, and the remaining thirty cars were made on chassis' supplied by Fiat. The main distinguishing feature of these vehicles were the stringed wheels of the Armstrong-Whitworth-Jarrot chassis and the rung wheels of the Armstrong-Whitworth-Fiat vehicles.

The Armstrong-Whitworth-Jarrot armored cars arrived in Russia between August and September 1915 and the Armstrong-Whitworth-Fiat cars between September 1915 and January 1916. The Russians realized that the Jarrots were not suitable for combat deployment. They recommended strengthening the Fiat's axles; their turrets were provided with boxy superstructures and armored wings were added to protect the machine gun loopholes. Because of these adjustments, the Armstrong-Whitworth-Fiats were attached to combat units at the turn of 1916-17.

Similar to the Austin armored cars, the Russian Army extensively deployed Armstrong-Whitworth-Fiat armored cars on the Eastern Front during WWI as almost all sides of the Russian Civil War did as well. The Czechoslovak Legion in Russia captured two vehicles of this kind: one was destroyed in early June 1918, and the second survived and was in use until 1920.

Courtesy of VHÚ

BASIC TECHNICAL DATA (ESTIMATED):

Crew	5	
Weight	5,3t	
Length	475cm	
Width	190-200cm	
Height	245cm	
Headroom	22cm	
Wheel base	350cm	
Turret	2	
Tires	920x120	
Performance	Engine gasoline	gasoline, 50 HP
	Maximum speed	50 km/h
	Range	250 km
Armor	Front	4-5 mm
	Sides	4-5 mm
	Bottom and roof	4,5 mm
	Turrets	4,5 mm
Armament	2x machine-gun Maxim 1910 caliber 7,62 mm	
	Munitions carried	6000 pieces

GARFORD

A prototype of this heavy armored car was developed in the autumn of 1914 in the Putilov factory, according to the specifications provided by Major General N.M. Filatov. This armored car was developed on the four-ton truck chassis of the American Company Garford Motor Truck Co. The driver and his assistant sat at the front; underneath them was a fuel tank. A machine gun compartment was housed in the center of the vehicle with two Maxim machine guns in sponsons on both sides. A revolving turret with a cannon mark 1910 next to the third Maxim machine-gun was situated on the rear of the car. A lever controlled from the cab driver could switch all four forward speeds back and one reverse became reverse facing forward. The chassis was overloaded, but any design shortcomings were overshadowed by its cannon armament.

The first vehicle was ready on 3rd May 1915 and thirty vehicles were completed in October of the same year. The Russian military deployed them far and wide on the Eastern Front. Two light machine-gun armored cars and one heavy cannon armored car Garford formed an armored car platoon.

The Russian Admiralty ordered the next eighteen machines in September 1915. These were designed to defend the land perimeter of the Naval Fortress of Peter the Great (the former city of Revel, now Tallinn, Estonia). The contract was completed in December 1917. These machines were also deployed on the Eastern Front.

The German Army captured several Garfords which saw combat both against Russians and in the German Civil War. After the outbreak of the Civil War in Russia, Garfords were used by both Red and White armies. The Poles captured three machines, which later served in the Polish Army during the 1920s. The Lithuanian Army used Two Garfords, and the Estonians, Romanians and Czechoslovaks used others. They were in use by the Red Army up to 1931, but the Germans captured several of them as late as 1941.

Courtesy of VHÚ

Courtesy of VHÚ

BASIC TECHNICAL DATA (ESTIMATED):

Crew	8-9	
Weight	8,6 t	
Length	570cm	
Width	230cm	
Height	280cm	
Headroom	?	
Wheel base	?	
Turret	?	
Armor	6,5 mm	
Load balancing	Front axle	?
	Rear axle	?
Performance:	Engine	petrol, air-cooled, 30 hp
	Content engine	?
	Engine speed	?
	Speed up	17 km/h forward
		3 km/h backward
	Range	120 km
Obstacles:	Addiction	?
	Trench	?
	Ford	?
Armament	3 machineguns Maxim 7,62mm	
	1 gun 76,2	
	Munitions carried	5000 pieces for machineguns in 20 belts
		44 rounds for gun

FIAT-IZHORSKI

On 21st February 1916, the Anglo-Russian Committee in London concluded a contract with branches of the Fiat company in the U.S. for the manufacture of ninety chassis' for several armored cars. According to the contract, the chassis' were to be delivered to Russia by 1st October 1916. The parent Fiat factory modified its standard chassis under this contract by doubling the rear wheels and installing a more powerful engine. These were known as Fiat type 55. The first series chassis arrived in Russia in the summer 1916.

Preparations were also made for the production of armored hulls at the Izhorski plant of the Russian Maritime Ministry. Construction of the prototype began at the end of September 1916. The vehicle had two turrets, with one machine-gun each and dual controls. The thickness of the armor was 7 mm on the vertical surfaces and 4 to 4.5 mm on the horizontal surfaces. The prototype was finished on 2nd December 1916 and between 3rd and 16th December the body of the vehicle underwent stress tests. Its powerful engine meant the car could achieve a maximum speed of up to 70 kilometers per hour on the road.

Courtesy of VHÚ

Production began at the Izhorski plant in January 1917. Regardless of the tumultuous events of spring and summer of that year, production proceeded without delay. On 4th October 1917, sixteen armored chassis were completely finished, and on twenty-five additional the work was nearly complete. By April 1918, the Izhorski plant made forty-seven armored cars of this type. Another twenty-seven vehicles were armored up to 1920.

The Fiat-Izhorski armored cars constituted the main segment of the armored units deployed in the Russian Civil War and were used by both the Red and Whites armies. The Germans captured at least one vehicle of this type in the spring of 1918. The Finns used three, and at least three were captured by the Poles who used them until the late-1920s. In the summer of 1918, the Czechoslovak Army seized at least five vehicles, all of which were probably passed on to the Russian White Army. The Fiat-Izhorski remained in the service of the Red Army until the early-1930s. Several armored hulls, placed onto the AMO chassis, took part in combat in 1941.

BASIC TECHNICAL DATA (ESTIMATED):

Crew	5	
Weight	5,3 - 5,5 t	
Length	?	
Width	190cm	
Height	250cm	
Headroom	27cm	
Wheel base	?	
Turret	?	
Tires	?	
Load balancing	Front axle	?
	Rear axle	?
Performance:	Engine	gasoline, FIAT 60x90, 60-72 horsepower
	Content engine	?
	Engine speed	?
	Speed up	70 km/h
	Range	140 km
Obstacles:	Addiction	up to 150
	Trench	?
	Ford	? 60 cm
Armament	2 machine guns Maxim 7,62mm	

BENZ

This is one of the first armored cars built for Russia. On 11th October 1911 the St. Petersburg branch of the German company Benz & Co. Rheinische Automobil- und Motoren-Fabrik Mannheim AG received a contract for the production of an armored car. An interesting feature of this order was its sponsor: the Directorate of the Eastern Section of the Amur Railroad purchased the armored vehicle for 11,500 rubles.

According to the Russian historians Mikhail Baryatinski, Maksim Kolomiyec and Sergey Zykov, the St. Petersburg branch of Benz built this armored car on the basis of a chassis belonging to an Omnibus. The vehicle was identified in available documents as an "armored bus Benz" and it was able to travel on the rails when guarding the Amur Railroad against local bandits and when travelling over long distances. Its armored plate consisted of a thickness equivalent to sixth dyumas (about 4.5 mm) and it weighed 120 puds (1978 kg). The armored car had a Benz two-cylinder engine of 35/40 HP and had a crew of up to six men. Surveillance of the Amur Railroad began in August 1912 and it was deployed around the city of Khabarovsk. After the outbreak of the First World War it was taken over by the Russian Imperial Military. The armored Benz was mobilized and sent to St. Petersburg but it never arrived after breaking down.

On the basis of available archival material, it is clear that in building this armored car the Petersburg branch of the Benz factory used the two-axle omnibus chassis type Benz-Gaggenau BL with a four-cylinder engine (35/40 HP/25.7 up to 29.4 kW). German and Russian designers replaced the lightweight bus superstructure with a full armored body. Thin armored plates were also attached to the inner body frame for added protection. German companies during the Second World War used a similar design.

Body armor plates were attached to an internal support frame by rivets with a countersunk head and screws. However, the steering controls, front axle, chain drive rear axle, vehicle suspension and both front single and rear double wheels were left unprotected.

Courtesy of VÚA-VHA

In photos from Omsk and the Urals in 1918, the extent of repairs and the reinforcement of the chassis can be clearly seen. The front steering wheel and rear drive axle correspond in appearance to the Italian truck FIAT type 15 or 18. Metal felly wheels were equipped with solid rubber rims instead of tires. Also, the front axle suspension has an Italian look. For example, in 1911, Benz produced a hanger with a round shoulder of a small radius, while the Italian FIAT factory suspension design had a large radius. This explains these distinct modifications. German spare parts for Benz-Gaggenau omnibuses were probably unavailable in Russia during the First World War and had to be replaced with accessible parts from the Italian FIAT, which were similar in size and structurally more robust.

Technical data is not known.

JEFFERY-POPLAVKO

Starting in 1915, Staff Captain Viktor Poplavko, commander of the 26th Machine Gun Truck Platoon of the Russian Army, experimented with an armored car, which he himself designed. A vehicle called CHARODEY ("Wizard") was built on the chassis of the American Jeffery Quad truck from the Thomas Jeffery Company. The high terrain performance of this truck led to the idea of a new armored fighting vehicle, which in addition to the driver and gunner, was also designed to carry ten storm troopers armed with kindjal knives, hand grenades and Mauser pistols. The armored car was designed to go through antipersonnel obstacles at the level of enemy trenches. Then the carried infantry would capture them. According to Poplavko, sections of these "Hannibal Elephants," counting thirty such vehicles each, should be a key to a successful offensive.

In May 1916, CHARODEY underwent tests at the 7th Army Chief Engineer and then again in June by the Commission for Armored Cars in St Petersburg. Following this, on 8th August 1916 the Commission ordered the first thirty vehicles from the Izhorski plant, which were completed at the end of September.

Courtesy of VÚA-VHA

Crew	4 (+10 carried men of shock infantry)	
Weight	cca 8 t	
Length	cca 4520 mm	
Width	cca 2000 mm	
Height	cca 2140 mm	
Headroom	cca 300 mm	
Wheel base	? 3150 mm	
Tires	?	
Load balancing	Front axle	?
	Rear axle	?
Performance:	Engine	gasoline, 32 horsepower
	Content engine	4725 ccm
	Engine speed	?
	Speed up	35 km/h
	Range	?
Obstacles:	Degree	up to 150
	Trench	?
	Ford	? 60 cm
Armament	2 machine gun Maxim, 4 loopholes	
Armor	7 mm	

The armored car had armor 7 mm thick, and it carried two Maxim machine guns, portable between four loopholes. The main weakness of this vehicle was the entrance door on the right side of the cab only, which left the crew trapped inside in case of tipping on to the right side.

The Special Purpose Armored Section was created on 10th September 1916. In addition to thirty Jeffery Poplavko armored cars, it had four passenger and four freight cars, four tank trucks, one workshop truck and nine motorcycles. Its commander was Staff Captain Poplavko. The Section arrived at the front on 16th October 1916. It was assigned to the 11th Army of the Southwest Front, however it was not deployed in its intended combat role. During the offensive in July 1917, the armored cars belonging to the Special Purpose Armored Section were deployed in a traditional role, and were not used to breakdown enemy field fortifications. During the retreat of the Russian Army from Tarnopol they covered the retreat of the main forces.

In the Russian Civil War, vehicles of this type were used on all fronts. The German Army used two machines captured at Tarnopol in street fighting in Berlin in 1919. In 1919, the Polish Army seized two machines as well. And the Czechoslovaks in Russia captured one machine of this kind, which later became known as JANOŠÍK.

BIANCHI

During the First World War, the Italian Company Fabbrica di Automobili e velocipede Edoardo Bianchi & C. produced more than 45,000 bicycles, 1,500 motorcycles and 1,000 cars of various designs. Three armored vehicles were built on a chassis produced by the company during 1913-16. Each armored vehicle was unique in design and used a different chassis.

The first model was built in 1913. It was equipped with a closed armored body and a rotating turret with a machine gun. Armored fenders for the rear wheels and armored discs with solid rubber tires were added to the front wheels in order to provide added protection. This model was known as "Bianchi 30 hp." The second variant model dated from 1915. It was also equipped with a closed armored body and a rotating turret with a machine gun, but was known by the name of the Bianchi company only. The third model dated from 1916 and had a machine gun with a shield in an open top armored body. It was known as Bianchi "Pallanza." All three types were withdrawn from service in the Italian Army in around 1923.

The Bianchi type armored car as used by the Czechoslovak Legion was manufactured in 1915. The vehicle was fitted with an auxiliary protective frame designed for destroying and diverting wire obstacles. The frame was formed from a steel strip, and was attached to the body armor with metal beams. Its armored body was fitted on the sides with attachment points for mounting plates and tools, and an auxiliary loophole in the rear.

BASIC TECHNICAL DATA (ESTIMATED):

Crew	4 men	
Weight	3090 kg	
Length	4,5 m	
Width	1,8 m	
Height	2,5 m	
Headroom	0,25 m	
Wheel base	3,4 m	
Turret	Æ 1,4 m	
Tires	?	
Load balancing	Front axle	1240 kg
	Rear axle	1850 kg
Performance:	Engine	gasoline, ? kW (30 k)
	Content engine	? dm3
	Engine speed	?
	Speed up	46 km/h
	Range	? km
Obstacles:	Degree	? m
	Trench	? m
	Ford	? m
Armament	2 machine guns	

Courtesy of VÚA-VHA

It had a petrol engine, four-stroke, four-cylinder, water-cooled, with a driven chain drive to the rear wheels fitted with a split axle, and leaf spring suspension. A solid front steering axle was also suspended by leaf springs, and a rotating cylindrical turret was located on the roof. It carried a machine gun in a simple mount. The turret itself had a circular elevation (360 angular degrees) and the mounted weapon had an elevation range of 30 degrees horizontal and between -7 to +30 degrees in the vertical angle.

It came equipped with two 6.5 mm machine guns, probably system Vickers-Terni. One machine gun was placed in the rotating turret. The second machine gun was placed in the loophole in the rear of the hull.

Composition of crew:
- Vehicle commander
- Driver, mechanic
- Gunner in the turret
- Assistant and gunner in the rear

The Bianchi armored car only served in the Czechoslovak Army for a few days before it was withdrawn in December 1918.

LANCIA IZ

The Italian company Giovanni Ansaldo & C. produced its armored cars on the Lancia 1Z chassis (chassis) produced by the Italian factory Fabbrica Automobili Lancia & Co.

Its closed armored body was placed on a lattice frame chassis. Armored fenders protected the tires, but in the case of Czechoslovak vehicles only the rear axle was protected. The vehicle was fitted with auxiliary structures designed for destroying and diverting wire obstacles. The protective frame consisted of two steel L-profiles fixed to the body armor on metal beams. At the rear of the vehicle an auxiliary loophole was placed in the hull.

It had a petrol engine, four-stroke, four-cylinder, water cooled, type Lancia 1Z and gearbox driven cardan drive rear undivided axle with doubled wheels. The front steering axle and rear drive axle were sprung by leaf springs attached to the frame of the vehicle.

Courtesy of VHÚ

BASIC TECHNICAL DATA (ESTIMATED):

Crew	4 men	
Weight	3090 kg	
Length	5,6 m	
Width	1,82 m	
Height	2,75 m	
Headroom	0,15 m	
Wheel base	3,35 m	
Turret	Upper	? m
	Lower	Æ 1,4 m
Tires	Pirelli, 935 x 135	
Load balancing	Front axle	1600 kg
	Rear axle	2350 kg
Performance:	Engine	gasoline, 26,5 kW (36 k)
	Content engine	4,94 dm3
	Engine speed	2200 per minute
	Speed up	60 km/h
	Return rate	5 km/h
	Range	400 km
Obstacles:	Degree	0,35 m
	Trench	0,8 m
	Ford	0,8 m
Armament	3 Machine-guns with 15000 rounds	

Two rotating turrets were located on the roof of the vehicle in a vertical concentric arrangement. The lower large diameter turret was fitted with two machine guns mounted in simple fork mounts, which fired through cutouts in the side of the turret. A smaller upper turret was placed on the roof of the bottom turret and was fitted with one machine gun. Both revolving turrets had a circular elevation of 360 angular degrees. Individual guns were elevated in a horizontal range of about 30 degrees, and on the vertical range between -7 to +30 degrees. The following production model was equipped with only a large turret fitted with two machine guns and a third machine gun was used from a loophole in the rear end of hull.

It came equipped with three Italian 6.5 mm machine guns, probably system Vickers-Terni (or Maxim-Terni). In the 1920s, the Czechoslovak vehicles were re-armed with the vzor 24 machine guns, and the Schwarzlose machine gun, adjusted for ammunition with a Mauser S caliber 7.9x57 mm.

Composition of crew:
- Vehicle commander, gunner in the top turret
- Driver, mechanic
- 2 gunners in the bottom turret

SOURCES AND LITERATURE

PRIMARY SOURCES

Central Military Archives - Military Historical Archive, fund Autopark Cs. army in Russia.

Central Military Archives - Military Historical Archive, fund Fotosbírka Čs. Legií.

Central Military Archives - Military historical archive, photo archive.

Kronika pluka útočné vozby 1. In 1928-1930 written by Joseph Hranáč and František Marek. Jindřich Bunc copy of 1988.

LITERATURE IN ENGLISH

David Bullock: *The Czech Legion 1914-20*. Osprey Publishing, ISBN 1-84603-236-9.

David Bullock: *The Russian Civil War 1918-21*. Osprey Publishing, ISBN 1-84603-271-7.

D. Bullock – A. Aksenov: *Armoured Units of the Russian Civil War - White and Allied*.

Osprey Publishing, ISBN 1-84176-544-9.

D. Bullock – A. Aksenov – P. Sarson: *Armored Units of the Russian Civil War - Red Army*. Osprey Publishing, ISBN 1-84176-545-7.

Victor M. Fic: *Revolutionary War for Independence & the Russian Question - Czechoslovak Army in Russia*. 1914-1918. South Asia Books, ISBN 0-88386-968-3.

Victor M. Fic: *Bolsheviks and the Czechoslovak Legion: The Origin of Their Armed Conflict*. South Asia Books, ISBN 0-8364-0218-9.

Victor M. Fic: *The Collapse of American Policy in Russia and Siberia 1918*. Columbia University Press, ISBN 0-88033-308-1.

Victor M. Fic: *The Rise of the Constitutional Alternative to Soviet Rule in 1918 - Provisional Governments of Siberia and All-Russia and Their Quest for Allied Intervention*. Columbia University Press, ISBN 0-88033-403-7.

Marian Hronský: *Struggle for Slovakia and the Treaty of Trianon 1918-1920*. Veda, Bratislava 2001, ISBN 80-224-0677-5.

Ch. K Kliment - V. Francev: *Czechoslovak armored Fighting Vehicles 1918-1948*. Schiffer, Atglen 1997, ISBN 978-0764301414.

B. Perret - A. Lord: *The Czar´s British Squadron*. Kimber & Company, London 1981. ISBN 0-7183-0268-0.

LITERATURE IN CZECH

J. Č. (Annonymous): *Automobilní park Čs. vojska na Rusi*. Naše vojsko roč. 5 (XIV.), č. 19, 1. 7. 1932, s. 208-209.

J. Čermák: *Boje pod Bachmačem a ústup z Ukrajiny*. Památník odboje, Praha 1923.

Dopravní místopisný lexikon Československé republiky. Ministerstvo pošt a telegrafů za účasti Ministerstva železnic, Praha 1928.

V. Francev: *Československé tanky, obrněná auta, obrněné vlaky a drezíny 1918-1939*. Ars-Arm, Praha 1993.

V. Francev - Ch. K. Kliment: *Československá obrněná vozidla 1918-1939*. Ares, Praha 1999.

J. Galandauer a kol.: *Slovník prvního československého odboje 1914-18*. Praha 1993.

O. Holub: *Československé tanky a tankisté*. Naše vojsko. Praha 1991.

Marián Hronský, Anna Krivá, Miloslav Čaplovič: *Vojenské dejiny Slovenska*. Bratislava, 1996.

T. Jakl: *Československé broněviky na Rusi*. HPM 2002, č. 2.

T. Jakl: *Obrněné automobily československých legií v Rusku 1918-1920. Sonda do problematiky*. In: *Československé legie a první světová válka, sborník*, Jihočeské muzeum, 2002, s. 46-57.

K. Kavena: *Dějiny dělostřeleckého pluku 1 Jana Žižky z Trocnova v ruské revoluci a ve vlasti*. Praha 1937.

Václav Klimeš: *Poslední cesta z Miškovce*. Italský legionář, ročník IV, číslo 1-2, 30. 04. 1934, s. 6 až 9.

Z. Klöslová: *Legionářská literatura – Korejci a Korea*. Nový Orient roč. 56, 2001, č. 2.

F. Kovanda: *Vzpomínka na boje na Slovensku*. Italský legionář, ročník VIII, číslo 2, 15. 12. 1937, s. 22-27.

K. V. Knobloch: *Válečný zápisník československého legionáře v Rusku*. Praha 1993.

J. Kopta – F. Langer – R. Medek: *Od Zborova k Bachmači*. Praha 1938.

B. Kuška: *U Lučence*. Italský legionář, ročník IV, číslo 1-2, 30. 04. 1934, s. 6-9.

V. Lahoda: *Historický pramen a obraz*. Dějiny a současnost 1991, č. 1.

F. Langer: *Pamětní kniha 1. střeleckého pluku Mistra Jana Husi*.

Legionáři Berounska. Beroun 2001.

Lexikon Slovenských dejín. Bratislava 1999.

M. Majtán: *Názvy obcí Slovenskej republiky*. Veda, Bratislava 1998.

R. Medek a kol.: *Za svobodu - obrázková kronika československého revolučního hnutí na Rusi 1914-1920*. I. -IV. , Praha 1925-1929.

P. Minařík: *Československý zahraniční vojenský odboj v letech 1914 - 18*. Veda - Armáda - Spoločnosť, 1992, č. 1, s. 99 - 129.

T. Pavlica: *Československé legie*. Obrana národa, roč. 2002.

R. Pitra: *Z Penzy do Ufy*. Praha 1922.

M. Pleský: *Dějiny 4. střeleckého pluku Prokopa Velikého 1917-1920*. Trutnov 1927.

J. Podobský: *Padova*. Italský legionář, ročník VIII, číslo 2, 15. 12. 1937, s. 22-27.

F. Prudil: *Legionářská odyssea*. Praha 1990.

R. Sak: *Anabáze - drama československých legionářů v Rusku (1914-1920)*. H&H, Jinočany 1996.

J. Tintěra-I. Bajtoš: *Legionářské obrněné automobily*. HPM 1993, č. 10.

J. Vacietis: *S vojáky revoluce*. Praha 1987.

V. Veber: *Komunistický experiment v Rusku 1917-1991 - Malé dějiny SSSR*. Praha 2001.

J. Vejnar: *Úderný prapor*. Praha 1930.

L. Wiesner: *Operace 3. střelecké divize ruských legií na sibiřské magistrále a přechod přes řeku Manu*. Vojensko-historický sborník II. (1933), sv. 2, s. 131-163.

A. Zeman (red.): *Cestami odboje – IV. díl*. Praha 1928.

LITERATURE IN RUSSIAN

М. Барятинский - М. Коломиец: *Бронеавтомобил Австин.* Бронеколекция 1997-01.

М. Барятинский - М. Коломиец: *Бронеавтомобили русской армии 1906-1917.* Техника молодёжи, Москва 2000.

М. Веллер, А. Буровский: *Гражданская история безумной войны.* АСТ, Астрель, Москва 2010.

М. Коломиец - И. Мощанский: *Бронеавтомобил Ланчия I3.* Бронеколекция 1998-04.

М. Коломиец: *Броня русской армии: бронемашины и бронепоезда Первой Мировой.* Эксмо, Москва 2010, ISBN 978-5-699-43085-7.

V. Шпаковский: *Железные гробы, италяанская бронетехника за свой первые 40 лет.* Техника и вооружение 1998-07.

О. V. Теребов: *Армии Деникина до и после разгрома.* Военно-исторический журнал 1996-04, 1996-06.

LITERATURE IN UKRAINIAN

А. Тири: *На периферії війни. Бельгійський бронедивізіон в Україні. 1916–1918.* Темпора, Киев 2010. ISBN 978-617-569-008-6

LITERATURE IN GERMAN

Benz-Gaggenau-Lastwagen. Der Motorwagen, roč. 1913, č. 19, s. 671.

Die deutsche Automobil-Industrie auf der Baltischen Ausstellung in Malmö. Der Motorwagen 1913, No. 17, p. 401-405.

W. Gebhardt: *Deutsche Omnibusse seit 1895.* Motorbuch Verlag, Stuttgart.

F. Heigel: *Taschenbuch der Tanks.* J. F. Lehmans Verlag, München 1926.

F. Heigel: *Taschenbuch der Tanks - Ergänzunsband.* J. F. Lehmans Verlag, München 1927.

H. Kaufhold-Roll: *Die deutschen Radpanzer im Ersten Weltkrieg.* Biblio, Osnabrück 1996, ISBN 3-7648-2468-9.

LITERATURE IN ITALIAN

R. Giovanelli - G. B. Tasca: *Dov'e la Patria mia? (La causa cecoslovacca e l'Italia)*. Societe Tipo-Editrice ravennate di mutilati, Ravena 1928.

LITERATURE IN POLISH

J. Magnuski: *Samochod pancerny Garford*. Militaria roč. 1, č. 1.

J. Magnuski: *Samochody pancerne wojska polskiego 1918-1939*. WiS, Warszawa 1993, ISBN 83-860-28-00-9.

INTERNET

Бронеавтомобили во Владивостоке 1919-1920. http://nektonemo.livejournal.com/2721860.html

M. Čaplovič: *Francúzska vojenská misia v ČSR 1919 – 1938*.
http://www.historiarevue.sk/hr03-02/nato/caplovic.htm

M. Hronský: *Talianska vojenská misia*.
http://www.historiarevue.sk/hr03-02/nato/hronsky.htm

J. Queisner: *Replika obrněného automobilu Austin JURÁŠ*.
http://www.austinjuras.estranky.cz

E. Sieche: *The Austro-Hungarian Danube Flotilla*.
http://www.gwpda.org/naval/danube.htm